The Spending Loop

Understanding Why We Buy and How to Finally Stop

Matthew Thomas

Disclaimer

What's written here comes from research, observation, and lived experience with spending patterns and systems that help manage them. Nothing here constitutes professional financial advice, therapy, or medical guidance. If you're dealing with compulsive spending that's creating serious harm, if you're hiding financial behavior from people in your life, or if money issues are part of larger mental health struggles, talking to a qualified professional makes sense.

The suggestions about automation, apps, and financial tools reflect what was available and functional at the time of writing. Technology changes, companies change their policies, what works shifts over time. Use what makes sense for your situation, ignore what doesn't, and adapt anything that needs adapting to fit your life.

References to specific products, apps, or services aren't endorsements or advertisements, they're just examples of tools that exist and that some people find useful. Always do your own research before connecting any app to your financial accounts or signing up for services that handle your money.

Acknowledgements

To everyone who has ever looked at their bank statement with genuine confusion about where the money went, who has felt shame about forgotten subscriptions or impulse purchases, who has tried every budget app and found themselves back where they started within weeks. Your patterns are valid, your struggles are real, and you're not alone in this.

To the researchers studying decision fatigue, dopamine systems, working memory, executive function, and all the cognitive processes that make financial management harder than it looks from the outside. Your work makes it possible to understand these patterns as neuroscience rather than character flaws.

To anyone who has ever said "I'm just bad with money" and meant it as fact rather than judgment. We're not bad with money, we just have brains that need different infrastructure, and that's a completely different thing.

Chasing the Click

It's 11:42 on a Tuesday night and you're already in bed, phone in hand, scrolling through a site you didn't intend to visit. You weren't even thinking about buying anything. Somehow a pair of shoes has appeared in your cart. By the time you click confirm, you feel great. By the time you wake up, you feel something else entirely. Three days later, the shoes arrive. You leave the box by the door for a week before opening it.

The feeling of clicking "buy now" is different from the feeling of receiving what we bought, and understanding that difference explains why we can order something at midnight, feel great about it for approximately fifteen minutes, wake up the next morning with buyer's remorse, and then find ourselves shopping again two days later even though the first package hasn't arrived yet. The satisfaction doesn't come from having the thing, it comes from the moment of acquisition, from the anticipation of getting it, and that distinction matters because it means we're chasing a feeling that evaporates almost immediately and has to be recreated over and over, which is exactly what makes impulse buying so hard to stop.

Dopamine is the neurochemical involved here, though not in the way most people think about it. It's not a pleasure chemical exactly, it's more accurately an anticipation and motivation chemical, the thing that makes us want to pursue rewards and that activates most strongly not when we get what we want but when we expect we're about to get it. When we're scrolling through a shopping site and we see something we like, when we're reading reviews and imagining how the product will improve our life, when we're adding it to cart and entering payment information, our brain is releasing dopamine in response to the anticipated reward. By the time we click "confirm purchase" we've already gotten most of the neurochemical payoff, which is why the high peaks before we even complete the transaction and starts declining almost immediately after.

This is why the package arriving feels anticlimactic more often than not, why we can be so excited about something when we order it and then barely care when it shows up three days later, why we sometimes don't even open boxes for days or weeks after delivery. The dopamine hit already happened, the reward system already activated and then returned to baseline, and the actual object can't recreate that anticipation high because anticipation is definitionally about something that hasn't happened yet. Once we have the thing, there's nothing left to anticipate, which means the neurochemical process that made us want it so badly is complete and we're back to our default state, which for many of us feels flat or restless or unsatisfying in a way that makes us want to recreate that dopamine spike by shopping for something else.

The cycle goes like this: we feel bad or bored or stressed, our brain looks for something that will provide relief or stimulation, shopping presents itself as an available option that's easy and immediately accessible, we start looking at products and the anticipation system activates, dopamine levels rise as we imagine having the item and solving whatever problem we think it will solve, we make the purchase and get a spike of satisfaction, the dopamine fades within minutes or hours, we're left with the original bad feeling plus often some guilt about spending money we maybe didn't want to spend, we feel worse, and the cycle is primed to repeat. This isn't a logic problem, it's a neurological loop that happens before our rational thinking catches up to what we're doing, and trying to stop it through willpower alone is like trying to stop being hungry through discipline. The drive is physiological, not just psychological.

The prefrontal cortex is the part of the brain responsible for rational planning, impulse control, evaluating consequences, and overriding emotional responses with logical thinking, and it's the brain region that would theoretically tell us "actually, we don't need another water bottle" or "maybe we should check our bank balance before buying this" or "let's think about whether we'll actually use this enough to justify the cost." The problem is that the prefrontal cortex is extremely sensitive to stress, and when we're stressed or tired or overwhelmed, its activity decreases while the activity in emotional and reward centers increases. This means exactly when we most need rational oversight of our decisions, our brain is least capable of providing it, and the parts of our brain that want immediate gratification are running the show without much interference from the part that thinks about long-term consequences.

By the time the prefrontal cortex realizes what's happening and tries to intervene, we've often already added three things to cart and entered our credit card information and clicked through to confirmation. The rational brain is slower than the emotional brain, it takes longer to process information and evaluate options and consider outcomes, and in the fast-moving context of online shopping where we can go from seeing a product to owning it in under two minutes, there's often not enough time for rational thinking to catch up before the transaction is complete. We make the purchase in an emotional or impulsive state, and only afterward, when the dopamine fades and the prefrontal cortex comes back online, do we realize we didn't actually want or need what we bought. But by then it's too late, the money is spent, and we're stuck with the object and the guilt.

What this looks like in practice varies, but the underlying mechanism is consistent. We buy things when we're stressed because the dopamine hit provides temporary relief from cortisol and overwhelm, even though the relief lasts maybe twenty minutes and then we're back to feeling stressed plus now we're worried about money. We buy things when we're bored because the stimulation of shopping activates our reward system in a way that feels better than understimulation, even though scrolling product pages doesn't actually address the understimulation problem and leaves us still bored but poorer. We buy things to celebrate because our brain associates rewards with positive events and shopping is an easy accessible reward, even though we're spending money that could go toward the actual thing we're celebrating. We buy things because we saw someone else have them and our brain translated that into "if I have this object I will have their life," even though objects don't work that way and we know that intellectually but the emotional brain doesn't care about intellectual knowledge.

We buy things because they're on sale, which is particularly insidious because it creates a sense of urgency and activates loss aversion, the fear of missing out on a deal is processed by our brain as an actual loss, and avoiding loss is more motivating than pursuing equivalent gain. A product that's 40% off triggers "if I don't buy this now I'm losing $30" thinking even though we're not losing anything, we just aren't getting a discount on something we might not have bought at full price anyway. The sale price makes the purchase feel financially responsible, we're saving money by spending it, which is exactly the cognitive distortion retailers want us to have because it bypasses our normal resistance to spending. Our emotional brain sees "save $30" and experiences that as a positive outcome, and the prefrontal cortex that would point out we're still spending $45 we wouldn't have spent otherwise doesn't get consulted until after the purchase is complete.

The particular challenge for people whose baseline dopamine runs lower than average is that they need more stimulation to feel normal, to reach the level of activation that other people experience from less intense activities. For someone whose dopamine system is naturally less active, maybe because of genetics or maybe because of ADHD or depression or other conditions that affect neurotransmitter function, normal activities don't provide enough stimulation to feel satisfying, which means we're constantly seeking sources of dopamine that are strong enough to register. Shopping provides a reliable hit, it's accessible from our phones at any time, it doesn't require leaving the house or coordinating with other people or having energy for something demanding, and it works quickly. The problem is that it's also expensive and unsustainable, but when our brain is desperate for dopamine, the long-term consequences don't feel relevant compared to the immediate need for stimulation.

This isn't about lacking willpower, it's about fighting a neurochemical process that's happening outside conscious awareness and that's specifically designed by evolution to motivate us toward rewards. The dopamine system exists because pursuing rewards was adaptive for survival, finding food and safety and mates all required motivation to search for them and pleasure when we found them, and our modern brain is still running software designed for that environment. The problem is that in the current environment, rewards are artificially abundant and accessible, we can get dopamine hits from clicking buttons on our phones instead of having to work for them, and our stone-age reward system doesn't know the difference between "found food that will keep us alive" and "bought decorative throw pillows we don't need." The mechanism is the same, the motivation and the chemical release happen regardless of whether the reward is actually beneficial, and we're stuck with a dopamine system that treats online shopping like it's survival-critical.

"Just stop" doesn't work because we're not dealing with a logic problem that can be solved through better information or stronger commitment. We're dealing with a neurochemical system that operates largely outside conscious control and that's specifically designed to override rational thinking when it detects possible rewards. Telling someone to use willpower to stop impulse buying is like telling someone to use willpower to stop their heart from beating faster when they're scared, the mechanism isn't under voluntary control in that way, and willpower is itself a limited resource that depletes under stress exactly when the dopamine system becomes most active. What we need instead of willpower are external systems that interrupt the cycle before the dopamine spike happens or that add enough friction that our rational brain has time to catch up before the purchase completes, but we'll get to systems later. First we need to understand all the ways our brains make this hard, because the dopamine problem is only one piece.

The Invisible Drain

You sit down to look at your credit card statement and something doesn't add up. Not one big thing — just a lot of small ones. A streaming service you haven't opened in four months. An app you downloaded once for a free trial. A membership you kept meaning to cancel. Each one is only a few dollars. Together, they've been draining money you didn't know you were spending.

The average person pays between $91 and $119 per month on subscriptions, which works out to somewhere between $1,092 and $1,428 per year, and 42% of people are paying for subscriptions they've completely forgotten about. Not subscriptions they're keeping despite not using them, but subscriptions they're not using because they don't remember the subscriptions exist. When researchers ask people to estimate their monthly subscription spending, the average person underestimates by $133, which means we think we're spending $50 when we're actually spending $183, and that gap between what we think we're paying and what we're actually paying is where a significant amount of our money disappears without us noticing.

This is not an accident, this is exactly how subscription business models are designed to work. The model depends on us signing up and then forgetting, on the friction of cancellation being high enough that even when we notice we're paying for something we don't use, we don't cancel it, on the individual amounts being small enough that they don't trigger serious scrutiny. Each subscription feels negligible when we sign up, "just $9.99 per month" is how it's always framed, and we fully intend to use it or cancel it after the free trial, but then it auto-renews and we don't notice because it's buried in a credit card statement we don't check carefully and the billing is paperless so there's no physical reminder arriving in the mail every month that would make us think about whether we still want it.

Subscription creep happens gradually enough that we don't register the accumulation. First we have Netflix, which feels completely reasonable, then we add Hulu because there's a show we want to watch, then Disney+ comes along and seems worth it for the catalog, then HBO Max has something we're interested in, then we add Spotify premium because ads are annoying, then we upgrade our iCloud storage because our phone keeps warning us we're running out of space, then we sign up for a meal kit service to make cooking easier, then we download an app that has a free trial and forget to cancel it, then we sign up for Amazon Prime for the shipping and now we're paying for Prime Video too even though we already have four streaming services. Each addition by itself seems justified or at least minor, but together they've ballooned into $100 or $150 or $200 per month, and we don't realize it because they're spread across multiple payment methods and bill at different times throughout the month and none of them alone feels like a financial problem.

What used to be one cable bill is now six streaming services plus Spotify plus iCloud storage plus three apps we forgot we were paying for plus that subscription box that seemed fun when we signed up but we haven't used in four months. The total is higher than the cable bill was, but it feels smaller because it's distributed across multiple charges that don't appear together in a way that would let us see the full cost. This is intentional design, companies know that unbundling services and charging separately makes people willing to pay more than they would for the same things packaged together, because our brains don't automatically sum up distributed costs the way we evaluate a single large charge.

Tracking subscriptions is genuinely hard, not just carelessness or lack of attention. They're spread across multiple credit cards, some are attached to PayPal or Apple Pay or Google Pay, some are buried in app store subscriptions that we access through phone settings rather than the regular billing interface, some are tied to email addresses we don't use anymore, and they all bill at different times throughout the month so there's no single point where we see everything at once and can evaluate the total. We'd have to go through every credit card statement, every digital wallet, every app store account, pull three months of data because some subscriptions bill quarterly or annually, and manually identify which charges are recurring versus one-time purchases, and that's assuming we remember all the places where we might have payment methods stored, which most of us don't.

The psychology of why we don't cancel even when we do notice is its own problem. Sunk cost fallacy makes us think "I've already paid for this month, I might as well keep it and get my money's worth," which doesn't make logical sense because whether we keep it or cancel it, the money for this month is already gone, but it feels wasteful to cancel something we've paid for. The hassle of cancellation is deliberately designed to be high enough that we'll choose to keep paying rather than deal with it, companies make signing up trivially easy and canceling intentionally difficult, sometimes requiring phone calls during business hours or navigating through multiple pages trying to convince us to stay or making the cancellation button hard to find. Optimism bias makes us think "I'll use it more next month" even though we haven't used it for six months and there's no actual reason to believe next month will be different, but we want to believe we'll become the kind of person who uses all their subscriptions efficiently and canceling feels like admitting that we're not that person.

The most commonly forgotten subscriptions are streaming services people signed up for one specific show and never cancelled after finishing it, food delivery subscriptions like DoorDash Plus or Uber Eats Pass that seemed useful when we were ordering frequently but now we're not, gym memberships that bill annually so we don't see the charge every month to remind us we're paying, app subscriptions buried in phone settings for apps we downloaded once to try a feature and then never opened again, magazine or news subscriptions that auto-renewed after a promotional period ended and jumped to full price without us noticing, software subscriptions for programs we used briefly for a project and then stopped needing. These aren't expensive individually, but $9.99 plus $14.99 plus $12.99 plus $4.99 plus $6.99 adds up to $49.95 per month, which is $599.40 per year, which is a significant portion of the emergency fund we keep saying we can't afford to build.

The real cost over time is what makes this particularly damaging. Fifteen dollars per month feels like nothing, it's the cost of two coffees, it's less than we spend on a single meal out, it doesn't trigger any mental alarm that says "this is a significant financial decision." But fifteen dollars per month is $180 per year, and when we have five of these it's $900 annually, and when we have ten it's

$1,800, and suddenly we're talking about real money that could go toward debt payments or savings or things we actually care about. The amounts are specifically calibrated to stay below the threshold where we'd think seriously about the cost, just low enough that canceling feels petty or not worth the hassle, but high enough that they generate substantial revenue for companies when multiplied across millions of subscribers who are all making the same calculation.

Companies know exactly what they're doing with this model. Recurring revenue is more valuable than one-time purchases because it's predictable and compounds over time, a customer who pays $10 per month for five years is worth $600 versus a customer who pays $50 once, and the math becomes even more favorable when you factor in that many subscribers will forget or not bother to cancel even after they stop using the service. The entire business model depends on psychological friction and memory failures, on making it easy to start and hard to stop, on keeping prices just low enough that the cost doesn't hurt enough to motivate cancellation. They win when we forget, when we're too busy to cancel, when we keep meaning to cancel but never actually do it, and they've optimized every part of the user experience to make those outcomes as likely as possible.

Our working memory is the cognitive system responsible for holding and manipulating information temporarily, and it has limited capacity that varies between people but is generally understood to be around four to seven items for most people, fewer for people with ADHD or other executive function differences. This is fine for many daily tasks, but it means we can't rely on our brain to keep track of every subscription we're paying for, especially when those subscriptions accumulate over months or years and when we're not regularly using all of them in a way that would keep them active in our memory. Something we signed up for eight months ago and used twice is not going to stay in our working memory, it's going to fade into the background and we'll forget it exists until we happen to notice the charge on a statement, if we notice it at all.

This is where the gap between intention and execution becomes obvious. We intend to keep track of our subscriptions, we intend to cancel things we're not using, we intend to review our statements regularly and catch unnecessary charges, but intention doesn't equal ability when the cognitive load exceeds our working memory capacity. We can't remember things our brain doesn't have the capacity to hold, and adding "remember all subscriptions" to our mental to-do list doesn't increase our working memory capacity, it just adds another item competing for limited cognitive resources. What we need instead of trying harder to remember is external memory systems that track subscriptions for us, which we'll get to in later chapters, but first we need to understand that this isn't a personal failure, it's a design problem where the system is built to exploit the limitations of human memory.

The forgetting problem compounds with the dopamine problem we talked about in the previous chapter, because the same neurochemical process that makes us want to sign up for subscriptions also makes us forget about them afterward. The dopamine hits when we're signing up, when we're imagining all the value we'll get from this service, when we're activating the free trial and feeling excited about access to new content or features. After we sign up, the dopamine fades, the excitement wears off, and the subscription becomes just another background charge that doesn't provide any emotional activation because we're not actively using it. Our brain filed it away as "handled" and moved on to other sources of dopamine, and unless something prompts us to think about it again, it will stay filed away while continuing to drain money from our account every month.

Running on Empty

By 9pm you've already made hundreds of small decisions: what to wear, what to eat, how to respond to that message, which route to take, whether to stay in the meeting or leave early. Your rational brain is winding down. This is exactly when the notifications arrive, when the sales feel most urgent, when the cart fills itself almost without you noticing.

Every decision we make throughout the day depletes a finite cognitive resource, similar to how physical activity depletes energy, and when that resource runs low our decision-making quality deteriorates in predictable and measurable ways. This is called decision fatigue, and it's not about being weak-willed or undisciplined, it's about a genuine depletion of the mental resources required for careful evaluation and impulse control. When we're fresh in the morning, we might carefully compare prices and read reviews and consider whether we actually need something before buying it, but by evening after we've made hundreds of decisions about what to wear and what to eat and how to respond to emails and which route to take to avoid traffic and whether to attend a meeting and what to prioritize at work, we're operating with significantly reduced capacity for that kind of careful deliberation.

The effects of decision fatigue show up in several ways that are all bad for our finances. We become more impulsive, choosing immediate gratification over better long-term outcomes because evaluating long-term consequences requires cognitive resources we've depleted. We start avoiding decisions entirely, which sounds like it would conserve energy but actually makes us more vulnerable to default options and to sales tactics that present themselves as the path of least resistance. We lose the ability to resist temptations that we could have easily dismissed earlier in the day, which is why the candy bar at the grocery store checkout is so dangerous after we've just spent an hour making decisions about which brand of pasta sauce to buy and whether the organic vegetables are worth the extra cost and which type of bread fits our current dietary intentions. Our capacity for self-regulation decreases with each choice we make, and by the time we're tired and depleted, we're making decisions with whatever scraps of willpower we have left, which is often not enough.

This shows up in our spending patterns in ways we can usually recognize once we start looking for them. We buy the candy bar or magazine or energy drink at checkout even though we went to the store with a specific list and those items weren't on it, but we've been making choices for the past hour and we're tired and it's right there and it's only a few dollars and we just want to be done shopping and get home. We add things to cart during late-night scrolling sessions when we should be sleeping but instead we're on our phones in bed, scrolling through product pages without any particular goal, and our defenses are completely down because we're exhausted and our rational brain has largely checked out for the day. We say yes to unnecessary upsells when making purchases because evaluating whether we actually need the extended warranty or the premium shipping or the add-on product requires more mental energy than we have available, and "just say yes" is easier than thinking through the value proposition.

We choose the default option even when it costs more because choosing requires comparing alternatives and weighing trade-offs and projecting future scenarios, and all of that is cognitively demanding in ways we can't manage when we're depleted. The default option presents itself as requiring no decision, even though accepting it is itself a decision, and our tired brain takes the path that feels like it requires the least additional thinking. This is why subscription services default to auto-renew, why shopping carts default to having items in them rather than being empty, why premium options are pre-selected in many checkout flows, companies know that when we're tired or overwhelmed we'll stick with whatever requires the least active choosing.

Shopping is particularly draining as an activity because it requires sustained attention and repeated micro-decisions that accumulate into significant cognitive load. Every product we look at, every specification we compare, every review we read, every price we evaluate against our budget, every feature we weigh against our actual needs, each of these is a small decision that draws from our finite cognitive resources. Online shopping makes this worse because the options are functionally infinite, we can comparison-shop across dozens of sites and hundreds of products, reading thousands of reviews and specifications, and there's no natural endpoint where we run out of things to look at or have to leave the store because it's closing. We can comparison-shop ourselves into such complete exhaustion that we either buy everything we looked at because we can't face making more decisions about what to eliminate, or we buy nothing and have to start the entire process over tomorrow when we've recovered, which means we go through the same draining cycle again.

The factors that make decision fatigue hit faster and harder compound on each other in ways that are particularly relevant to modern life. Choice overload happens when we're faced with too many options, and research consistently shows that more choices don't make us happier or help us make better decisions, they make us more anxious and more likely to avoid deciding or to make poor decisions just to be done with the process. Twenty varieties of yogurt at the grocery store sounds like it should be good because we can find exactly what we want, but in practice it means we have to evaluate twenty options when we probably only care about three or four decision factors, and the cognitive cost of processing all those options is higher than the benefit of having marginally more choice.

Cognitive overload happens when we're trying to process too much information at once, and this is endemic to online shopping where every product page has specifications and features and compatibility information and size charts and materials lists and care instructions and customer questions and answers and related products. Our working memory can only hold a limited amount of information at once, somewhere around four items for most people, and when we're trying to compare products across multiple dimensions while also keeping our budget in mind and remembering what we already own and considering how this purchase fits with our other priorities, we're asking our working memory to juggle far more than it can handle. The result is that we either make snap decisions based on incomplete evaluation, or we get paralyzed and can't decide at all, or we make decisions and then second-guess them because we couldn't hold all the relevant information in mind at once while deciding.

Stress from other parts of life depletes our decision-making capacity even before we start shopping, so if we've had a difficult day at work or a conflict in a relationship or unexpected bad news or just the accumulated stress of managing responsibilities and obligations, we're already starting from a depleted baseline. Adding shopping decisions on top of that stress means we're making financial choices with even less cognitive resource available than usual, which is why stress shopping is such a common pattern. We turn to shopping when we're stressed because it provides temporary relief, but we're also making those purchases in exactly the mental state where our decision-making is most compromised, which means we're more likely to buy things we don't need and will regret later.

Physical tiredness affects our cognitive function in ways that mirror mental fatigue, so if we're physically exhausted from not sleeping enough or from doing demanding physical work or from being sick, our ability to make careful decisions decreases even if we haven't been making a lot of choices. The brain requires energy to function properly, and when we're physically depleted we have less energy available for cognitive tasks including the kind of careful evaluation that prevents impulse purchases. This is why shopping when we're tired is dangerous, not because we're not trying hard enough but because our brain literally doesn't have the resources to evaluate purchases carefully.

Time pressure creates additional stress that further depletes our decision-making capacity, so when we're rushing or when we feel like we need to decide quickly, we're more likely to make poor choices or to default to impulse rather than careful thought. This is why limited-time offers and countdown timers are such effective sales tactics, they create artificial time pressure that makes us decide quickly using whatever decision-making capacity we have left, which if we're already tired or stressed or overwhelmed, is not much. The urgency bypasses the careful evaluation we might do if we had time to think about the purchase without pressure, and companies know this, which is why they manufacture urgency even for products that aren't actually scarce or time-limited.

The concept of the "poor tax" is relevant here because people with less money have to make more careful trade-offs with every purchase, which means more decisions, which means more decision fatigue, which means less willpower left to resist impulse purchases by the time they reach the end of shopping. Someone with abundant resources can buy the more expensive option without thinking hard about it, but someone on a tight budget has to weigh whether the cheaper option is good enough or whether spending more is worth it for better quality, has to calculate whether buying in bulk saves money in the long run or whether they can't afford the higher upfront cost, has to decide whether this purchase means giving up something else they need. Every purchase requires active decision-making instead of being automatic, and that decision-making depletes resources that then aren't available for resisting impulse purchases.

The person who's trying to figure out how to feed their family on $50 for the week is making vastly more decisions than the person who can buy whatever looks good without checking prices, and by the time they get to checkout with their carefully calculated cart, they've exhausted their decision-making capacity and are more vulnerable to the impulse candy purchase or the magazine or the lottery ticket. This isn't about poor people having less willpower, it's about poor people having to spend more cognitive resources on basic survival decisions, which leaves them with less capacity to resist temptation. The very act of being careful with money is cognitively expensive in ways that make it harder to continue being careful with money, which is part of why poverty is so difficult to escape, it's not just about having less money, it's about having to make more decisions with less cognitive resource available.

Evening is particularly dangerous for spending because we've been making decisions all day about everything from what to eat for breakfast to how to handle a problem at work to what to say in a difficult conversation, and by the time we're sitting on the couch scrolling through our phones at nine or ten at night, we're operating with whatever scraps of decision-making capacity we have left after a full day of depletion. This is exactly when we're most likely to be on social media seeing things we want to buy, or browsing shopping sites because we're bored and tired and looking for something mildly stimulating, or getting ads targeted to our interests because algorithms know this is when we're most vulnerable. Our rational thinking is compromised, our impulse control is depleted, and we're making financial decisions in exactly the mental state where we're least equipped to make good ones.

The combination of all these factors means that by the time we're shopping in the evening after a stressful day where we've made dozens or hundreds of decisions and we're physically tired and mentally depleted and being presented with choices and urgency and social proof, we're basically defenseless against tactics designed to get us to buy. We might have been able to resist in the morning when we were fresh, we might have carefully evaluated whether we need something and decided against it, but by evening we don't have the cognitive resources for that kind of evaluation and we're making decisions based on what feels easiest or most immediately satisfying, which is usually clicking buy. This isn't a personal failure, it's a predictable result of cognitive depletion meeting deliberately engineered sales psychology, and knowing that doesn't make us immune but it does help us understand why we need external systems that don't rely on our depleted evening willpower.

They Know Exactly What They're Doing

The countdown timer says the offer ends in 43 minutes. The product page shows only 3 left. Someone in Portland just bought one. You weren't planning to buy anything tonight. But now you're entering your card number.

The tactics companies use to get us to buy things are designed by people who understand psychology better than we do, who have access to data about what works on different types of people in different contexts, who test and optimize every element of the buying experience to maximize the percentage of people who complete purchases. We're not competing against our own willpower, we're competing against teams of psychologists and data scientists and user experience designers whose entire job is figuring out how to overcome our resistance to spending, and they're very good at what they do because companies pay them enormous amounts of money to be good at it. Accepting that we're up against this kind of professional expertise helps remove the shame of falling for these tactics, we're not stupid or weak, we're just individuals trying to resist systems that are specifically engineered to exploit our psychological vulnerabilities.

Urgency manufacturing is one of the most common and effective tactics, creating artificial time pressure that makes us decide quickly without careful evaluation. Countdown timers showing "offer ends in 47 minutes" make it seem like we need to act immediately or lose the opportunity, even though in many cases the same offer will be available tomorrow or next week or the timer will reset after it reaches zero. Low stock alerts claiming "only 2 left at this price" trigger fear of missing out and scarcity psychology, even though the website might show "only 2 left" continuously for weeks as inventory gets replenished. Notifications that "someone in Seattle just bought this" create social proof and urgency simultaneously, suggesting that the product is popular and moving quickly and we should buy now before it's gone, even though the notification might be completely fabricated or based on a purchase that happened days ago.

All of these tactics work on the same underlying mechanism: they trigger emotional responses that bypass rational evaluation. When we see a countdown timer, our brain registers urgency and scarcity, and the emotional centers that respond to potential loss activate before the rational centers that would evaluate whether the urgency is real. By the time we think "wait, is this actually a limited-time offer or is this timer just going to reset," we've often already clicked through to checkout because the emotional impulse moved faster than rational thought. This is the same prefrontal cortex delay we talked about in Chapter 1, the rational brain is slower than the emotional brain, and urgency tactics are designed to exploit that gap by making us act on emotion before reason catches up.

Confirm shaming is the practice of making the option to decline feel embarrassing or irrational, using manipulative copy on decline buttons that says things like "no thanks, I'd rather pay full price" or "I don't want to save money" or "I don't care about my family's safety." This makes us feel stupid or cheap or irresponsible for not buying, triggering an emotional reaction that has nothing to do with whether we actually want or need the product. Our brain experiences the shame as real even though we intellectually know it's a manipulative tactic, and for many people the emotional discomfort of clicking the shameful option is strong enough that they'll buy just to avoid feeling bad about themselves. The companies using these tactics know they're manipulative, that's why they work, they're deliberately triggering negative emotions that make us choose purchase over the psychological discomfort of being judged by a website button.

Social proof appears everywhere in modern commerce because it's extremely effective at influencing behavior. "Emma from Austin just saved hundreds" creates the impression that real people are getting value from this purchase, even though we don't know Emma, we don't know if she actually saved money or just spent money, and the testimonial might be completely fabricated. Influencer validation makes products seem desirable because people we admire or aspire to be like are using them, even though influencers are usually being paid to promote products and their endorsement doesn't mean the product is actually good or that it will work for us. Customer reviews provide social proof that other people bought and liked the product, but we often don't stop to consider that negative reviews might be filtered out, positive reviews might be incentivized or fake, and the people writing reviews might have completely different needs and preferences than we do.

"Trending now" labels create herd mentality, suggesting that if everyone else is buying this then we should too, even though popularity doesn't equal quality or value and what's trending changes constantly based on algorithmic manipulation rather than genuine organic interest. The underlying psychological principle is that humans are social animals who look to others for guidance about what to do, and in uncertain situations we default to doing what we see other people doing. Companies exploit this by manufacturing the appearance of social consensus, making it seem like everyone is buying their product when actually they're just very good at creating that impression through strategic use of social proof signals.

Platform-specific manipulation varies based on the interface but serves the same goal of making purchases easier and more frequent. Amazon's one-click ordering removes the friction that might give us time to reconsider, we go from seeing a product to owning it in a single click, and that's by design because Amazon knows that any additional steps between intent and purchase create opportunities for us to change our minds. Personalized recommendations based on browsing history feel helpful, like the site is showing us things we're interested in, but they're actually showing us things we're most likely to buy based on data about what products correlate with purchases for people with similar browsing patterns. The goal isn't to help us find what we need, it's to show us things we didn't know we wanted until we saw them, creating new desires that lead to new purchases.

"Frequently bought together" suggestions create the impression that other shoppers have found value in these combinations, but they're often based on purchase correlations that might be meaningless or might be the result of other people falling for the same suggestion. If the site shows "customers who bought this also bought X," some percentage of those purchases happened because people saw that exact suggestion and decided to follow it, which means the correlation is self-reinforcing rather than reflecting genuine need. We see the suggestion, assume it must be useful if other people are buying these items together, buy both items, and become part of the data that reinforces the suggestion for the next person, creating a cycle where the suggestions become true through repetition rather than through actual utility.

TikTok Shop combines entertainment with embedded purchasing in a way that's particularly effective because we're watching videos that activate our emotions and then the option to buy appears right there while we're emotionally aroused from the content. We see someone using a product, we feel entertained or inspired or amused, and before that feeling fades we can click to purchase without ever leaving the app or having time for the rational brain to engage. The friction between seeing and buying has been reduced to almost nothing, and the emotional activation from the video content primes us to make impulse purchases that we wouldn't make in a neutral emotional state. The entire design is optimized for conversion, turning viewers into buyers as efficiently as possible by removing anything that might interrupt the path from watching to purchasing.

Instagram makes aspirational lifestyles look attainable through purchase by showing us carefully curated images of people who seem to have their lives together, who have beautiful homes and fashionable clothes and interesting experiences, and then showing us the specific products that supposedly enable that lifestyle. We see someone living a life we want, our brain creates a connection between their life and their possessions, and we start to believe that buying the same things will help us achieve the same lifestyle, even though we know intellectually that objects don't work that way. The aspirational content creates desire, the shopping integration makes fulfilling that desire immediate and easy, and we end up buying things in pursuit of a lifestyle that the products themselves can't actually provide.

The subscription business model is designed specifically to maximize recurring revenue while minimizing cancellations, and every element of the user experience reflects that goal. Signing up is trivially easy, usually requiring just email and payment information and maybe a password, taking less than two minutes from landing on the site to having an active subscription. Canceling is deliberately difficult, requiring us to log in, navigate through multiple pages, often declining several offers to stay at a discounted rate, sometimes having to call during business hours or chat with a retention specialist whose job is to convince us not to cancel. The asymmetry is intentional, companies know that if they make canceling as easy as signing up, more people will cancel, so they add friction to the cancellation process while removing friction from signup.

Price increases are hidden in fine print or mentioned in emails we don't read carefully, so we signed up for $9.99 per month and six months later we're paying $14.99 without really noticing because the charge is automatic and we're not reviewing our statements carefully. The monthly amount is kept small enough that we won't think canceling is worth the effort, even though we're not using the service, because $12 or $15 per month doesn't feel like enough to justify the hassle of canceling. This is carefully calibrated, too expensive and people would cancel, too cheap and the company doesn't make enough money, and the sweet spot is the amount where we think "I should cancel that" but never actually do it because it doesn't seem urgent or important enough to prioritize.

Email marketing uses psychology at every level, from subject lines designed to create urgency or curiosity to personalization that makes the email feel like it's specifically for us rather than a mass mailing. Subject lines like "your cart is waiting" or "don't miss out" or "ends tonight" create fear of missing out and motivate us to open the email and click through. Personalization using our name or referencing products we've looked at makes the email feel more relevant and harder to ignore, even though the personalization is automated and happening at scale across millions of recipients. Abandoned cart reminders come with additional discounts, rewarding us for not completing our initial purchase and training us to abandon carts deliberately to get better prices, which companies know but accept because the conversion rate from abandoned cart emails is high enough to justify the discount.

"We miss you" messages when we haven't shopped in a while create emotional connection to a brand that's just trying to get us to spend money, making it seem like they care about our absence when actually they just want to reactivate us as a customer. All of this is timed based on data about when we're most likely to open emails and click through and make purchases, so we're getting these messages at the times when we're most vulnerable to their influence. Morning emails arrive when we're checking our phone before getting out of bed and our defenses aren't up yet, evening emails arrive when we're tired and depleted and more susceptible to impulse, weekend emails arrive when we have more time to browse and shop.

Algorithms learn our weaknesses by tracking every interaction we have with their platform and using that data to optimize their approach to getting us to spend more. They know when we buy, whether we're more likely to purchase in the morning or evening or on weekends, they know what triggers purchases for us specifically, whether it's sales or new arrivals or social proof or scarcity messaging. They know how much we're willing to spend on different categories of products, they know what kind of products we can't resist even when we're trying to save money, they know how long we typically browse before buying and can use that information to time their interventions. They know if we buy when stressed or bored or late at night, and they know to show us more tempting products during those times because we're more likely to convert.

This level of optimization is only possible because of the data we generate with every click and view and search and purchase, data that companies aggregate and analyze to understand patterns and correlations that we're not aware of in our own behavior. We might not realize that we always buy when stressed or that we're more likely to purchase after viewing product videos or that we respond strongly to certain types of social proof, but the algorithms know because they've tracked thousands of our interactions and found the patterns. They use this information to show us exactly the right product at exactly the right time in exactly the right way to maximize the chance we'll buy, and we're not aware this is happening because the optimization is invisible, we just see what seems like a normal shopping experience that somehow consistently results in us buying more than we intended.

This isn't about being smarter than marketing or seeing through these tactics so they don't affect us, because these tactics are designed to work even on people who understand them. Knowing that countdown timers are artificial doesn't stop them from creating urgency, knowing that social proof might be fabricated doesn't stop it from influencing our perception of value, knowing that personalization is automated doesn't stop it from making emails feel more relevant. The psychological mechanisms these tactics exploit are largely automatic and pre-conscious, they trigger responses before our rational brain can intervene, and even when we're aware of what's happening we're still vulnerable because awareness alone doesn't disable the response.

What we need instead of trying to be immune to marketing is accepting that we're up against professional expertise and enormous resources and sophisticated data analysis, and we need external systems to counter that rather than relying on our individual willpower and awareness. We need to remove ourselves from marketing channels entirely by unsubscribing from emails and unfollowing brands and deleting shopping apps, we need to add friction to purchases so our rational brain has time to catch up to emotional impulses, we need to automate savings so money is protected before we're exposed to spending temptations. The goal isn't becoming someone who can resist any marketing tactic, the goal is reducing our exposure to marketing and building systems that compensate for our vulnerability when we are exposed, recognizing that this is an infrastructure problem that requires infrastructure solutions rather than a personal strength problem that requires us to just try harder.

Stop Trying Harder, Start Building Smarter

Every January, the advice is the same: make a budget, track your spending, just be more disciplined. Every February, the budget is abandoned. Not because you don't care. Because willpower runs out, and no amount of caring replaces it when it's gone.

The willpower myth tells us that managing money is fundamentally about self-discipline, that if we just tried harder and cared more and made better choices we'd be financially stable, and this myth persists despite overwhelming evidence that willpower is an unreliable foundation for any behavior change that needs to last longer than a few weeks. Treating spending problems as discipline problems assumes we can decide to be better and then execute perfectly through pure force of will, but willpower is a finite resource that gets depleted by stress, by decision fatigue, by basically everything else happening in modern life, and we can't rely on willpower we don't have. When we're tired or stressed or overwhelmed or have already made too many decisions that day, our willpower is already gone, and telling ourselves we should have more of it doesn't make it magically appear.

What external systems do is make the right choice the default choice or the automatic choice, removing the need for repeated decision-making and willpower expenditure every time we're faced with a financial decision. The decision gets made once when we're thinking clearly, when our prefrontal cortex is fully online and we can evaluate options rationally, and then the system executes that decision without requiring ongoing mental effort or self-control. We decide once to move $200 to savings every payday, set up the automatic transfer, and then it happens every two weeks without us having to remember or choose or resist the temptation to spend that money instead. We decide once that we're not going to shop between 8pm and midnight because that's when we're most vulnerable, install a browser extension that blocks shopping sites during those hours, and then the decision is enforced by the system rather than requiring us to resist temptation every single evening.

Automation for money takes several forms, all built on the same principle of making financial decisions once and then having systems execute them without ongoing input. Bill payments happen automatically so we can't forget and incur late fees that add unnecessary cost and damage our credit score, and the automation removes the mental load of remembering due dates and initiating payments, which for people with executive function challenges can be the difference between paying on time and paying late with penalties. Savings transfers move money to savings the day after our paycheck arrives, before we see it sitting in our checking account looking spendable, and this timing matters because money we never see in checking doesn't register as available for spending in the same way that money sitting there does. Investment contributions happen without us thinking about it, whether that's 401k contributions taken directly from our paycheck or automatic transfers to investment accounts, removing the monthly decision about whether we can afford to invest this month and just making it happen regardless.

Debt payments that are scheduled and nonnegotiable mean we're making progress without having to maintain motivation and discipline month after month, and the automation is particularly valuable for debt because paying down debt doesn't provide the same immediate gratification as spending does, which makes it hard to prioritize using willpower alone. When the payment is automatic we don't have to choose debt over something more immediately satisfying, the choice has already been made and the system executes it. This doesn't mean we should automate everything without paying attention, we still need to monitor accounts to make sure automation is working correctly and that we're not overdrafting, but the day-to-day execution happens without requiring our active involvement.

Why this works especially well for certain brains is that people who struggle with executive function, which includes abilities like planning, organization, time management, working memory, and sustained attention, benefit disproportionately from automation because it removes the need for abilities we don't consistently have. The system doesn't forget, it doesn't get distracted, it doesn't lose track of time, it doesn't get overwhelmed by competing priorities, it just executes the instruction we gave it when we set it up. For someone whose working memory doesn't reliably hold onto bill due dates or savings goals, automation means those things happen anyway without depending on memory. For someone whose attention gets pulled in multiple directions and struggles to maintain focus on long-term goals, automation means progress happens without requiring sustained attention. The system compensates for what our brain struggles with, which is exactly what external systems should do.

The "pay yourself first" principle is built into automated savings transfers, and the psychology here is that money that goes to savings before we see it in checking doesn't feel like sacrifice because it was never available to spend in the first place. We adjust our spending to what's available in checking rather than spending everything and trying to save what's left, and for most people what's left is nothing because money expands to fill available space. If we have $2000 in checking after bills, we'll find ways to spend close to $2000, but if we have $1500 in checking because $500 went to savings automatically, we'll adjust and find ways to live on $1500. This isn't about deprivation, it's about working with how our brain actually perceives available money, which is not as "total money owned" but as "money visible in the account we spend from."

The timing of the transfer matters significantly, setting it for the day after payday rather than the day before next payday means we're working with behavioral economics principles about present bias and temporal discounting. Money that's close to payday feels less spendable because we know more money is coming soon, money that's far from payday feels more available because we're not thinking about whether we'll have enough to last until the next paycheck. Transferring money to savings right after payday means we're removing it when it feels least necessary, when we just got paid and our checking account looks full and we're not worried about running out. By the time we might miss that money later in the pay period, it's already gone and we've adjusted our spending around its absence.

Separate accounts serve as a practical structure for mentally separating different kinds of money and removing decisions about where money should go. One checking account for bills and necessary expenses with enough buffer to avoid overdrafts, one checking account for discretionary spending with a set amount per week or per month that we can spend without guilt because it's designated spending money, savings accounts for specific goals with clear labels like "emergency fund" or "vacation" or "car replacement," investment accounts for long-term that we think of as locked and unavailable for current spending. Each account has a single purpose, which reduces the cognitive load of evaluating every transaction against multiple competing priorities, we know that money in the discretionary account is for spending on whatever we want and money in the emergency fund is not available for dinner out no matter how much we want it.

The multiple account structure also creates friction for accessing certain types of money, which is protective when our impulses are trying to raid savings for non-emergencies. If our savings is in a separate bank from our checking, not linked to our debit card, requiring a transfer that takes a day or two to complete, that's enough delay that many impulses will fade before we can act on them. We might really want to buy something in the moment, but if accessing the money requires logging into a different bank and initiating a transfer and waiting two days for it to clear, by the time the money is available we've often moved on and no longer want the item. This isn't about making it impossible to access our own money, it's about making it inconvenient enough that we only do it when we genuinely need to rather than on impulse.

Physical barriers to spending work on the same principle of adding friction between impulse and purchase, recognizing that the ease of modern spending is exactly what makes it hard to control. Deleting shopping apps from phones means we can't buy from those retailers during idle moments when we're bored or waiting or scrolling without purpose, and having to open a browser and navigate to the website adds just enough friction that some impulses fade before we complete the purchase. The Amazon app is particularly dangerous because it's designed for maximum frictionless purchasing, we can go from seeing a product recommendation to owning it in under a minute, and removing that app creates necessary delay. Food delivery apps go for the same reason, if we have to open a browser and navigate to the delivery site we're more likely to just make food at home, which is both cheaper and often healthier.

Store apps in general should be evaluated skeptically, they exist because retailers know that having an app on someone's phone increases purchasing frequency, they can send notifications that trigger shopping behavior, they can make buying easier through saved payment information and one-click ordering, and they generate data about our habits and preferences that feeds into targeted marketing. Unless we're actively using an app for something specific like checking prices while in the store, having it on our phone is probably costing us money. Deleting it removes the temptation and the notifications and the ease that leads to impulse purchases.

Deleting saved payment information from browsers and websites means one-click ordering is no longer possible, every purchase requires entering payment information manually, and that creates a pause between impulse and completion that lets rational thinking catch up. This is deliberately annoying, that's the point, the annoyance is protective because it gives us time to reconsider whether we actually want what we're buying. When we have to pull out our credit card and type in the number and expiration date and security code, we're creating multiple opportunities to ask ourselves "do I actually need this" or "can I afford this" or "am I just buying this because I'm bored," and sometimes the answer makes us close the tab without completing the purchase. The companies removing this friction know exactly what they're doing, they're removing opportunities for us to change our minds, so putting the friction back is a reasonable defense.

Browser extensions that block shopping sites give us control over when we can access these sites, and we can use that control to protect ourselves during vulnerable times. Tools like Cold Turkey, Freedom, or StayFocusd let us schedule blocks during certain hours, limit time on specific sites, or block sites entirely until we manually unblock them with enough friction that it's not casual. We can block shopping sites from 8pm to 8am if we know evenings are when we're most likely to impulse shop, we can limit ourselves to 15 minutes per day on Amazon if we find ourselves browsing endlessly, we can block sites entirely during high-stress periods when we know our impulse control is compromised. This isn't about never shopping, it's about choosing when we're allowed to shop based on when we're most capable of making good decisions.

Physical card strategies create literal barriers to accessing payment methods, making impulse purchases require enough effort that the impulse often fades before we can act on it. Keeping credit cards in a drawer at home instead of in our wallet means we can't use them while we're out, we have to be home and make a conscious decision to get the card, which is enough delay that many impulse purchases don't happen. Freezing credit cards in a block of ice is extreme but effective for people who need maximum friction, if we have to wait for the ice to thaw before we can use the card, that's hours of delay during which most impulses will completely dissipate. Putting a sticky note on the card that says "do you actually need this" or "check your bank balance first" creates a moment of forced reflection before we can use it.

Using debit cards instead of credit cards creates real-time consequence of depleted checking balance, which for some people is more effective than credit cards where the consequence feels distant and abstract. When we use a debit card we see our checking balance drop immediately, which makes the cost feel more real than credit card spending that we'll deal with later when the bill comes. The downside is that debit cards have less protection against fraud and don't build credit, but for people who struggle with credit card debt, switching to debit can be a useful tool for making spending feel more concrete and immediate.

Unsubscribing from marketing emails removes triggers that prompt us to go look at things and potentially buy them, and the cumulative effect of removing these triggers is significant even though each individual email seems harmless. Every promotional email is an opportunity for retailers to get us onto their website where we're exposed to products and sales and recommendations and all the psychological tactics we discussed in the previous chapter, and even if we don't buy something this time, they're keeping themselves present in our mind and increasing the likelihood we'll think of them next time we want something in their category. Unsubscribing removes us from that cycle, we stop getting prompted to shop when we weren't thinking about shopping, and the reduction in exposure reduces spending.

The process takes five minutes per email but pays off in reduced temptation over time, and we should unsubscribe rather than just deleting emails because they'll keep coming and we'll have to make the decision to delete them over and over, whereas unsubscribing makes the decision once and then we stop getting the emails. Most marketing emails have an unsubscribe link at the bottom, clicking it takes us to a page where we confirm we want to unsubscribe, and we're done. Some retailers make this deliberately harder by requiring us to log in or by presenting multiple options about email preferences rather than a simple unsubscribe button, but it's still worth the effort because each unsubscribe removes an ongoing source of spending temptation.

Unfollowing influencers and brands on social media is harder emotionally because it can feel like we're missing out or being judgmental of people we like, but if seeing someone's lifestyle or possessions makes us want to shop, unfollowing them is self-protection. Social media is designed to make us want things, influencer content is advertising even when it's not technically sponsored, and if our response to seeing certain content is feeling inadequate with what we have and wanting to buy things to close that gap, we need to stop seeing that content. This isn't about judging the influencers or the brands, it's about recognizing that their content is triggering spending behavior we're trying to reduce and removing that trigger from our feed.

We can appreciate that someone creates content we enjoy and also recognize that following them is costing us money, and those two things can both be true simultaneously. The decision isn't about whether they're good or bad, it's about whether following them is compatible with our financial goals, and if it's not, unfollowing is the right choice for us even if other people can follow them without it triggering spending. This is about our brain and our patterns, not making universal judgments about content.

The cart trick satisfies the impulse to acquire without requiring immediate purchase, we add items to cart to scratch the itch of wanting to buy something, but we don't complete the purchase right away. The act of adding to cart provides some of the dopamine hit we're seeking, it feels like we're moving toward having the item even though we haven't spent money yet, and for many people that's enough to satisfy the immediate urge. We can come back tomorrow or next week and look at what's in our cart with fresh eyes and a clear head, and often we'll remove things that no longer seem necessary or that we realize we don't actually want enough to spend money on.

Abandoned cart emails will come trying to lure us back with discounts, and we should ignore them rather than clicking through, because the discount is designed to trigger the fear of missing out and the feeling that we're getting a deal, both of which bypass rational evaluation. If we want something enough that we'd buy it without the discount, we can go back and buy it, but responding to abandoned cart emails trains us to abandon carts deliberately to get discounts, which defeats the purpose of using the cart as a pause mechanism. The cart is meant to create distance between impulse and purchase, not to become a negotiation tactic with retailers.

Shopping lists created in advance become the authority on what we're allowed to buy, removing in-the-moment decisions about whether we need things. We write the list when we're thinking clearly, not when we're in the store being bombarded with displays and endcaps and sale signs, and we stick to the list religiously because the list is boss, not our impulses while shopping. This requires discipline in a different way than resisting temptation requires discipline, we're not fighting an urge in the moment, we're following a rule we set for ourselves when we were capable of thinking clearly. The list removes the decision, we buy what's on the list and nothing else, and that clarity eliminates the mental negotiation about whether we need something or whether it's a good deal or whether we should get it just in case.

Pre-deciding removes in-the-moment choice, which is valuable because in-the-moment choice is when we're most vulnerable to impulses and marketing and decision fatigue. The list represents our priorities and needs as evaluated when we were calm and rational, and trusting that evaluation over our current impulses usually leads to better outcomes. This works for groceries and household items and anything else where we can plan ahead, though it's less applicable to discretionary purchases where spontaneity is part of the appeal, but even there we can have rules like "if it's not on my wishlist I don't buy it" or "I can only buy discretionary items on the first Saturday of the month," creating structure that limits impulse while allowing some room for wants.

Avoiding shopping when vulnerable is about recognizing our patterns and choosing not to expose ourselves to temptation during times when we know we're not equipped to resist it. If we know we buy when stressed, stressed is not the time to go to Target or browse online, we need to do something else that doesn't involve spending, go for a walk or call a friend or watch something or exercise or make something, any activity that interrupts the shop-impulse pattern. If we know we buy when bored, bored is not the time to open shopping apps or browse sales, we need other sources of stimulation that don't cost money. The impulse will pass if we don't act on it immediately, urges peak and then subside within minutes if we ride them out, and having alternatives planned in advance means we have something to do instead of shopping when the urge hits.

Accountability structures add external motivation when internal motivation isn't sufficient, telling someone else what we're trying not to buy or giving them visibility into our checking account or using apps that share spending data with an accountability partner. External eyes add social pressure that helps when our own resolve is weak, we're less likely to make an impulse purchase if we know someone else will see it and ask about it, and that slight increase in friction can be enough to prevent purchases we'd regret. This requires choosing the right accountability partner, someone who will be supportive rather than judgmental, who will ask questions rather than shame us, who we trust enough to be honest with about our struggles. The accountability shouldn't feel punitive, it should feel like having a teammate who's helping us achieve goals we've said we want to achieve.

Look at the Numbers

The number on the screen is higher than you thought it would be. Not catastrophically higher — just enough to make you feel a low, familiar dread. You had a rough sense of where your money was going. You were wrong. Now you have to decide whether to keep looking or close the tab.

We avoid looking at our spending patterns when we suspect they're bad because confronting the reality of how much we're spending and where it's going creates shame and anxiety, and in the moment avoiding those feelings is easier even though avoidance makes the problem worse by preventing us from taking any action to change it. The audit isn't about judgment or proving to ourselves that we're bad with money, it's about gathering information that's necessary for building systems that work, and we can't build effective systems without understanding our actual spending patterns rather than what we think or hope our patterns are. This process is uncomfortable, seeing concrete evidence of money wasted on subscriptions we forgot about or purchases we regret triggers genuine emotional pain, but sitting with that discomfort is required for change because we can't fix problems we won't look at.

The basic process is pulling two to three months of bank and credit card statements, enough time to capture patterns and recurring charges but not so much data that we get overwhelmed and give up before finishing. We download statements as PDFs or spreadsheets or look at them in online banking, and we go through line by line highlighting every transaction that isn't immediately obvious, every charge where we can't instantly remember what it was for or why we bought it. This immediately shows us how much of our spending is invisible to us, how many charges are going through that we're not consciously aware of, which is often much higher than we expect. We thought we knew where our money was going, but seeing it itemized reveals gaps between perception and reality.

Categorizing spending into buckets helps us see patterns rather than getting lost in individual transactions, and the categories should reflect our actual life rather than using predetermined categories from budgeting apps that might not match how we think about money. Housing, transportation, food, subscriptions, shopping, entertainment, and miscellaneous covers most spending for most people, but we can add or adjust categories based on what makes sense for our situation. The goal is understanding where money is going in aggregate, whether we're spending $400 per month on food or $800, whether subscriptions are $50 or $200, whether shopping is a major category or a minor one, because this information tells us where we have the most opportunity to reduce spending if we want to.

Looking for patterns rather than individual purchases means we're trying to identify what triggers spending and what categories are surprisingly high, not beating ourselves up about that one time we bought something expensive. Patterns are things like "I buy when I'm stressed" or "I order food delivery multiple times per week" or "I have a lot of small charges that add up" or "I keep buying stuff for hobbies I don't actually do." These patterns are actionable, we can build systems around them, whereas individual transactions are just data points that don't tell us much about our overall behavior. We're looking for the recurring themes that explain why money leaves our account the way it does.

Focus particularly on recurring charges and categories that are surprisingly high, because these represent ongoing drains that we can address through system changes rather than one-time spending decisions. A category being surprisingly high means our mental model of our spending doesn't match reality, we thought we were spending less than we are, and that gap is where money is disappearing without us noticing. Recurring charges are particularly important because they compound over time, a charge that happens every month for a year is twelve times more impactful than a single purchase of the same amount, and many recurring charges are things we signed up for and forgot about rather than things we're actively choosing to keep paying for.

Finding hidden subscriptions requires multiple approaches because they're distributed across different payment methods and platforms in ways that make them hard to track. We search email for keywords like "subscription," "billing," "renewal," "auto-renew," "thank you for your order," using our email search function to pull up every message that might be related to a subscription or recurring purchase. This catches subscriptions that are billing paperlessly, where we're not seeing a physical bill or even necessarily a notification every time they charge us, and email is often the only record that these subscriptions exist. We look for confirmation emails from when we signed up, renewal notifications we ignored, billing receipts we archived without reading, all of which contain information about subscriptions we might have forgotten.

Checking phone app store subscription settings reveals subscriptions that are billing through Apple or Google rather than directly from the service provider, and these are particularly easy to forget because they don't show up as separate charges on credit card statements, they appear as "Apple" or "Google" charges that don't specify what we're subscribing to. On iPhone we go to Settings, tap our name, then Subscriptions, and we see every subscription that's billing through our Apple account with the cost and renewal date. On Android we open Google Play Store, tap our profile icon, then Payments and Subscriptions, then Subscriptions. Looking at these lists often reveals apps we downloaded months ago for a free trial and never cancelled, services we meant to use but haven't, subscriptions we didn't even realize were subscriptions when we signed up.

Looking at credit card merchant names for recurring charges means going through statements and identifying any merchant that appears multiple times, because multiple appearances usually means a recurring subscription or a place we're shopping too frequently. We might see Netflix and Spotify and Hulu, which we expect, but we also might see charges from services we don't recognize because the billing name doesn't match the service name. "AMZN Mktp" is Amazon, but it's not always obvious, and many subscription services use billing names that are company names or payment processor names rather than the service name we know, which is part of how they stay hidden. When we see a recurring charge from a merchant we don't recognize, we search the merchant name online to figure out what it is, and often we discover subscriptions we completely forgot existed.

Using apps like Rocket Money or Truebill automates much of this process, these apps scan our bank and credit card accounts and identify recurring charges and subscriptions automatically, categorizing them and showing us the total monthly cost. They work by connecting to our financial accounts with read-only access and using algorithms to identify patterns that suggest subscriptions, and they can catch things we'd miss doing manual searches because they're looking at thousands of transactions across multiple accounts simultaneously. The apps aren't perfect, they sometimes identify regular purchases as subscriptions or miss actual subscriptions that don't fit their patterns, but they're a useful starting point that's faster and more comprehensive than manual searching, and many of them offer features to cancel subscriptions directly from the app rather than having to navigate to each service's website and deal with their cancellation process.

What to look for specifically once we have our list of subscriptions and spending patterns compiled: subscriptions we forgot about entirely, where seeing them listed is the first time we've thought about them in months and we realize we're not using them at all. Duplicate subscriptions for similar services, like having both Hulu and Netflix and HBO Max and Disney+ when we really only watch one or two of them regularly. Services we signed up for a free trial and never cancelled, where we meant to evaluate whether they were worth keeping and never got around to it so now we've been paying for months. Memberships we intended to use but don't, like gym memberships we visit twice a year or Amazon Prime when we rarely shop on Amazon anymore or premium tiers of services when the free version would be sufficient.

Apps we downloaded once and got charged for, often because the free version was limited and we upgraded to get some feature and then never used the app again but the subscription kept billing. Purchases that happen so regularly we don't notice them anymore, like daily coffee or frequent food delivery or weekly Target runs that have become such routine spending that we don't consciously register them as choices we're making. Small charges that individually seem insignificant but add up to substantial amounts when we sum them, the $3 here and $5 there and $8 somewhere else that accumulate into $200 or $300 per month we weren't aware of spending.

The emotional part of auditing our spending is unavoidable, seeing hundreds of dollars per month going to things we don't use or need feels terrible, and the instinct is to close the statement and pretend we didn't see it, go back to not knowing because not knowing is more comfortable than confronting waste and missed opportunities. Sitting with the discomfort anyway is necessary because this information is what enables change, we can't cancel subscriptions we don't know we have, we can't reduce spending in categories we don't realize are high, we can't adjust our behavior based on patterns we haven't identified. The discomfort is temporary, the changes we make based on this information will improve our financial situation permanently, and that tradeoff is worth it even though the process feels bad in the moment.

We should expect to feel shame or frustration or regret when we see our spending laid out, and those feelings don't mean we're doing something wrong, they mean we're confronting reality rather than avoiding it. The shame comes from the gap between how we want to be handling money and how we actually are handling it, and acknowledging that gap is the first step toward closing it. We can feel bad about money we've wasted while also recognizing that beating ourselves up doesn't help, what helps is taking the information we've gathered and using it to build better systems going forward. The past spending is already done, we can't get that money back, but we can prevent future waste by acting on what we've learned.

Categorizing without judgment means we're not labeling spending as "good" or "bad" but rather as "necessary," "valuable to me," "not sure why I have this," and "definitely don't need this." This removes the moral dimension and focuses on functionality and personal value, which is more useful for decision-making than guilt. Necessary spending is things we need to live, rent and utilities and groceries and transportation to work, and this category is relatively fixed though we might find ways to reduce it. Valuable spending is things that improve our life in ways we care about, maybe that's a streaming service we actually use heavily or a subscription that supports a hobby we genuinely engage in or regular purchases that bring us real satisfaction, and keeping these is fine because they're providing value that we've consciously decided is worth the cost.

"Not sure why I have this" is the middle category where we need to evaluate more carefully, these are things that might have been valuable at one point or that we thought would be valuable when we signed up but we're not sure if they still are, and this category requires us to be honest with ourselves about whether we're actually getting value or whether we're keeping something out of habit or optimism that we'll use it more in the future. "Definitely don't need this" is the clear category for cutting, subscriptions we forgot about or services we never use or purchases we regret, and these should be eliminated immediately because they're pure waste, money leaving our account for no benefit whatsoever.

The surprising categories for many people aren't big purchases but accumulated small charges that individually seemed insignificant, we're not spending recklessly on expensive items, we're bleeding money through hundreds of small transactions that we didn't think about because each one felt too minor to worry about. Six dollars here for coffee, fifteen dollars there for lunch, twenty-three dollars for something we saw online, eight dollars for a streaming service, twelve dollars for an app subscription, nine dollars for delivery fees, four dollars for convenience items at the store, and suddenly we've spent four hundred dollars without any single purchase that seemed like it required serious consideration. This is the reality for many of us, we're not making catastrophically bad financial decisions, we're making hundreds of slightly careless small decisions that compound into serious money.

Understanding this pattern is valuable because it means we don't need to make dramatic lifestyle changes, we just need systems that help us reduce or eliminate some of the small charges that aren't adding much value. Maybe we don't need to cut all coffee spending, but cutting it from daily to twice a week saves $100 per month. Maybe we don't need to cancel all subscriptions, but canceling the three we're not using saves $35 per month. Maybe we don't need to stop shopping entirely, but not buying small convenience items impulsively saves $80 per month. Small reductions across multiple categories add up to significant savings without requiring us to feel deprived or to change our lifestyle dramatically.

What to do with the information once we have it depends on the category and our confidence about value. Immediate cuts for things we definitely don't use or need, canceling forgotten subscriptions and stopping spending that's clearly wasteful, these changes are straightforward and should happen as soon as we identify them because there's no downside to cutting spending that's providing zero value. Evaluation for things in the middle, where we need to track over the next month whether we actually use something or whether we just think we might use it, setting a reminder to check back in thirty days and make a decision based on actual usage rather than hypothetical future usage. Keeping things that genuinely add value even if they cost money, because the goal isn't to cut all spending, it's to cut spending that doesn't align with our priorities and values, and some subscriptions or purchases are worth the cost if they're improving our life in ways we care about.

Building systems to prevent future subscription creep means creating rules and structures around signing up for new subscriptions, like requiring ourselves to cancel an existing subscription before adding a new one, or setting a hard limit on total subscription spending per month, or maintaining a list of active subscriptions in a visible place so we're constantly aware of what we're paying for. When we sign up for a free trial, we immediately set a calendar reminder for the day before it ends with a note about whether we want to keep it, and if we don't act on that reminder the default is cancellation rather than keeping it. We use virtual credit cards for subscriptions so we can cancel them instantly by canceling the card number rather than having to navigate cancellation processes, and we check our subscription list quarterly to verify we're still using everything we're paying for.

The annual review becomes part of regular maintenance, doing this audit process once per year even if we think we have our subscriptions under control, because subscription creep happens gradually and we need regular check-ins to catch it before it becomes significant. We pick a specific date, maybe January first or our birthday or the start of the fiscal year, whatever date is memorable enough that we'll actually do it, and we go through the entire process again, pulling statements and identifying subscriptions and evaluating whether they're still valuable. Annual review catches subscriptions that were valuable when we signed up but no longer are because our interests or situation changed, services we're keeping out of habit rather than active use, new subscriptions that accumulated over the year that we haven't evaluated as a group.

Adjusting systems as needed is part of the ongoing process, what works this year might not work next year as our life circumstances or spending patterns change, and we need to be willing to modify our systems when they stop serving us.

Maybe automation that worked when we were single doesn't work when we're living with a partner and sharing expenses, maybe blocking shopping sites that worked when we were stressed doesn't work now that stress has reduced but we still want to be able to shop occasionally. Systems aren't meant to be permanent and rigid, they're meant to be functional tools that we adjust when they stop functioning well, and regular review is how we identify when adjustments are needed and what form those adjustments should take.

Put Up Some Walls

You deleted the app once before. You redownloaded it three days later because you needed to check one thing. Within a week you were back to the same patterns. This chapter is about why the app keeps winning — and what you can actually do about it.

The entire infrastructure of modern commerce is designed to make spending as frictionless as possible, to remove every obstacle between seeing something and owning it, and this frictionlessness is exactly what makes controlling our spending so difficult because our brains don't have time to engage rational thinking before the transaction completes. What we need is to deliberately add friction back into the purchasing process, creating obstacles and delays that give our prefrontal cortex time to catch up to our emotional impulses, and while this feels counterintuitive in a world that celebrates convenience and speed, friction is protective when our natural impulse control isn't sufficient to prevent spending we'll regret.

Removing shopping apps from our phones is the single most impactful change many people can make because it eliminates the ability to shop during idle moments when we're bored or waiting or scrolling without particular purpose, times when we're most vulnerable to impulse purchases because we're understimulated and looking for something mildly engaging. If the app isn't on our phone, we can't browse products while sitting on the couch or lying in bed or waiting in line, and having to open a browser and navigate to the website manually adds just enough friction that some impulses fade before we complete the purchase. The Amazon app is particularly dangerous because it's optimized for maximum purchasing efficiency, one-click ordering means we can go from seeing a product recommendation to owning it in under thirty seconds, and that's not enough time for rational evaluation of whether we need it or can afford it or will actually use it.

Food delivery apps create similar problems, they make ordering restaurant food so easy that we do it multiple times per week when we would have made food at home if the friction had been higher, and the accumulated cost of frequent delivery adds up to hundreds of dollars per month that could have been spent on groceries or saved. Having to open a browser and navigate to the delivery site manually, having to re-enter our address and payment information every time, creates enough inconvenience that we're more likely to just make food at home because the effort of ordering feels disproportionate to the benefit. This isn't about never ordering delivery, it's about making it inconvenient enough that we only do it when we genuinely want it rather than defaulting to it because it's the easiest option available.

Store apps in general should be evaluated with skepticism about whether they're helping us or helping retailers extract more money from us, because these apps exist specifically to increase purchasing frequency and average order value through notifications, personalized recommendations, and reduced friction. Unless we're actively using an app for something specific like checking prices while shopping in person or accessing coupons we specifically want, having it on our phone is probably costing us money through impulse purchases triggered by notifications or by the ease of buying when we're bored. Deleting these apps removes the constant prompting to shop, removes the notifications that interrupt our day with sales and deals and new arrivals, removes the saved payment information that makes buying too easy.

The psychological impact of not having shopping apps is underestimated, it's not just about removing convenience, it's about removing a source of constant temptation and prompting that we're exposed to dozens of times per day. Every time we unlock our phone and see the app icons, we're being reminded that shopping is available, and for people whose brains seek dopamine hits through acquisition, that reminder is a trigger even when we weren't thinking about shopping before we saw the icon. Removing the apps removes the visual trigger, and over time this reduces the frequency with which shopping occurs to us as something to do when we're bored or stressed or have five minutes between activities.

Deleting saved payment information from browsers and websites means every purchase requires manually entering card details, and this creates multiple checkpoints where we can ask ourselves whether we actually want to complete this transaction. One-click ordering is designed specifically to bypass the moment of reflection that might lead to abandoning the purchase, removing the friction between impulse and completion so thoroughly that we don't have time to reconsider. When we have to pull out our credit card and locate it in our wallet and type in the sixteen-digit number and the expiration date and the three-digit security code and our billing zip code, we're creating four or five separate moments where we might think "actually, do I need this" or "can I afford this right now" or "am I just buying this because I'm bored," and any of those moments might be enough to make us close the browser tab instead of completing the purchase.

This is deliberately annoying, we're making our own life less convenient on purpose, and that annoyance is the entire point because convenience is what's making us spend money we don't want to spend. The companies that removed this friction know exactly what they're doing, they studied how many people abandon purchases when they have to enter payment information versus when it's already saved, and they removed the friction specifically because it increases conversion rates. Putting the friction back is us deciding that conversion rates aren't in our interest, that we'd rather have lower purchasing frequency even if it means more inconvenience when we do deliberately choose to buy something. The annoyance protects us from ourselves, and that's a worthwhile tradeoff when the alternative is hundreds of dollars in impulse purchases per month.

Browser extensions that block shopping sites give us technological enforcement of rules we set for ourselves, and this external enforcement is more reliable than trying to follow rules through willpower alone because the extension doesn't get tired or stressed or depleted the way our willpower does. Tools like Cold Turkey, Freedom, or StayFocusd let us block specific websites entirely, or block them during certain hours, or limit the amount of time we can spend on them per day, and once we set up these rules the extension enforces them without requiring our ongoing involvement. We can block shopping sites from 8pm to 8am if we know that evening is when we're most likely to impulse shop, creating a technological barrier that prevents access during our vulnerable hours even if we actively want to shop in the moment.

Limiting time on shopping sites to fifteen or twenty minutes per day prevents the endless browsing that often precedes impulse purchases, we can look at what we came to look at but we can't scroll for hours getting progressively more tempted by recommendations and related products and sales. Blocking sites entirely during high-stress periods when we know our impulse control is compromised means we're protecting ourselves during the times when we most need protection, and we can unblock them later when we're in a better mental state and capable of making more careful decisions. The key is setting up these blocks when we're thinking clearly, when our rational brain is fully online and can set rules that serve our long-term interests, and then letting the technology enforce those rules when we're not in a state to make good decisions.

The ability to override these blocks varies by tool, some require us to type out a long phrase or wait through a delay or restart our computer, and this friction is intentional because it means overriding isn't casual. If we really want to access a blocked site we can, but we have to deliberately choose to bypass the protection we set up for ourselves, and that deliberate choice is often enough to make us reconsider whether we actually want to shop or whether we're just acting on impulse. The override option means we're not completely locked out in case of legitimate need, but the friction of overriding prevents casual impulse purchases that would have happened if the site were immediately accessible.

Physical card strategies create literal distance between us and our payment methods, making purchases require enough effort that many impulses dissipate before we can act on them. Keeping credit cards in a drawer at home instead of in our wallet means we can't use them while we're out shopping, we'd have to go home specifically to get the card, and that extra trip creates hours of delay during which most impulses will completely fade. We might really want to buy something while we're at the store, but by the time we drive home and get the card and drive back, we've had enough time for the emotional intensity of wanting it to decrease and for rational thinking to engage, and often we decide we don't actually need it enough to make the return trip.

Freezing credit cards in a block of ice is extreme but genuinely effective for people who need maximum friction and who struggle with online shopping from home where going to get the card doesn't require leaving the house. If we have to wait for a block of ice to thaw before we can access our card, that's several hours of forced delay, and very few impulses survive several hours of waiting. This also creates a visual reminder every time we open the freezer that we're trying to control our spending, that we found it necessary to literally freeze our payment methods to prevent ourselves from using them impulsively, and that reminder can reinforce our commitment to reducing spending. The method sounds ridiculous and it is ridiculous, but ridiculous methods that work are better than sensible methods that don't, and for some people this is what's required to break the cycle of impulse purchasing.

Putting a sticky note on credit cards that says "do you actually need this" or "check your bank balance first" or "wait 24 hours" creates a moment of forced reflection before we can use the card, and even though we wrote the note and we know what it says, reading it in the moment of wanting to buy something activates our rational brain and prompts us to actually ask the question rather than just reaching for the card automatically. The note interrupts the automatic behavior pattern that goes from wanting something to buying it without conscious evaluation, inserting a pause where we have to acknowledge the question and formulate an answer, and sometimes that's enough to prevent purchases we'd regret.

Using debit cards instead of credit cards creates immediate visible consequence of spending because our checking balance drops right away, and for some people seeing the account balance decrease in real time makes spending feel more concrete and painful than credit card spending where the consequence feels distant and abstract. When we use a credit card we're spending money we'll deal with later when the bill comes, and "later" doesn't trigger the same emotional response as "right now," which is why credit card spending tends to be higher than debit spending for the same person. Debit cards show us the impact immediately, we can see our available balance shrinking, and if we're operating close to our limits that visible shrinkage can be enough to make us reconsider whether we can afford this purchase.

The downside of debit cards is that they have less protection against fraud than credit cards, if someone steals our debit card information they're accessing our actual money rather than a line of credit, and recovering stolen funds can be harder and slower. Debit cards also don't build credit history the way credit cards do, which matters if we're trying to establish or improve our credit score. But for people who have significant credit card debt or who consistently overspend on credit cards because the spending doesn't feel real, switching to debit can be a useful tool even with these downsides, because the immediate feedback of seeing our balance decrease makes us more careful about spending.

Unsubscribing from marketing emails removes hundreds of spending triggers per month, each promotional email is an opportunity for a retailer to get us thinking about their products and potentially to get us onto their website where we're exposed to all the psychological tactics designed to convert browsing into purchasing. Even if we don't click through on most emails, they're keeping the brand present in our mind and keeping shopping as an available activity in our mental catalog of things we could do when we're bored. Every "sale ending tonight" subject line, every "new arrivals you'll love" preview, every "complete your purchase" reminder is a prompt to think about shopping when we might not have otherwise, and the cumulative effect of removing these prompts is that shopping occurs to us less frequently as something to do.

The process of unsubscribing takes dedicated time but pays ongoing dividends, we need to go through our email and find every retailer or brand that's sending us promotional content and click the unsubscribe link at the bottom of their emails. Some emails make this easy with a clear unsubscribe button, others bury it in small text or require us to log in to our account to manage email preferences, and some deliberately make it confusing by offering multiple preference options instead of a simple "stop sending me emails" button. We should persist through the deliberately difficult ones because they're usually the retailers who send the most frequent and aggressive marketing, and unsubscribing from them has the highest payoff in reduced temptation.

We need to actually click unsubscribe rather than just deleting the emails or marking them as spam, because deleting means they'll keep coming and we'll have to make the decision to delete them every single time, whereas unsubscribing makes the decision once and then we stop receiving them. Marking as spam sometimes works but often doesn't because promotional emails we signed up for aren't technically spam, and some email providers don't treat them as spam even if we mark them that way. Unsubscribing is the only reliable way to stop the flow, and once we've unsubscribed from our major retailers and brands, we can maintain the unsubscribed state by immediately unsubscribing from any new promotional emails we receive rather than letting them accumulate.

The reduction in email volume is noticeable within days, our inbox stops being constantly full of sales and deals and new products, and the mental quiet that comes from not being constantly marketed to is surprisingly pleasant. We're not thinking about shopping as often because we're not being prompted to think about it multiple times per day, and this reduction in mental presence translates directly into reduced spending because we can't buy things we're not thinking about. Some people worry they'll miss important sales, but the reality is that sales happen constantly and we're not actually missing anything, there will always be another sale, and the cost of knowing about every sale is being exposed to constant spending triggers that cost us far more than we save by catching deals.

Unfollowing influencers and brands on social media is emotionally harder than unsubscribing from emails because it can feel like a personal rejection of people whose content we genuinely enjoy, but if following someone is triggering spending behavior we're trying to reduce, we need to protect ourselves by removing that trigger from our feed. Social media platforms are designed to keep us scrolling and to serve us content that generates engagement, and for many of us aspirational lifestyle content generates engagement by making us want things, want to redecorate our homes or upgrade our wardrobes or buy products that will supposedly make our lives more beautiful or efficient or interesting. The platforms show us more of what we engage with, so if we're stopping to look at home decor or fashion or product reviews, we'll get more of that content, which triggers more wanting and more spending.

Influencer content is advertising even when it's not technically sponsored, influencers make money by converting their audience into customers either through direct sponsorships or through affiliate links or through building personal brands that sell products. Their job is to make us want things, to make products look appealing and necessary and like the key to achieving the lifestyle they're presenting, and they're very good at their jobs because that's how they earn their living. When we see someone with a beautiful organized home, our brain creates a connection between their organizational products and having our life together, even though we know intellectually that buying container store products won't fix our executive function challenges. The emotional brain makes the connection anyway, and then we find ourselves shopping for organizers we don't need and won't use effectively.

We can appreciate someone's content and recognize that following them is incompatible with our financial goals, and both of these things can be true simultaneously without it being a judgment of the influencer or their content. The decision to unfollow is about us and our patterns and our vulnerability to certain types of triggers, not about whether they're creating good content or whether other people should follow them. Some people can follow aspirational lifestyle content without it triggering overspending, their brains don't make the same connections ours do between seeing beautiful things and needing to acquire beautiful things, and that's fine for them. For those of us whose brains do make those connections, unfollowing is self-protection, not judgment.

The same applies to brands, following brands on social media means volunteering to be marketed to, brands post new products and sales and behind-the-scenes content specifically to keep themselves present in our minds and to trigger desire for their products. Unless we have a specific reason to follow a brand, like we need to stay updated on a product we use regularly for practical reasons, following them is just exposing ourselves to additional marketing that we're trying to avoid in other areas of our life. We're unsubscribing from their emails and deleting their apps specifically to reduce exposure to their marketing, and continuing to follow them on social media undermines those efforts by maintaining a direct channel for them to market to us.

The cart trick works by satisfying the impulse to acquire something without requiring immediate purchase, we add items to our cart when we want to buy them and then we close the browser or app without checking out. The act of adding something to cart provides a small portion of the dopamine hit we're seeking, it moves us closer to having the item even though we haven't spent money yet, and for many impulses that small satisfaction is enough to take the edge off the wanting so we're not obsessively thinking about the purchase. We can come back to our cart tomorrow or in a few days and look at what we added with fresh eyes and a clearer head, and very often we'll look at items and think "why did I want this" or "I don't actually need this" or "this isn't worth the money," and we'll remove them without purchasing.

The items that stay in our cart after multiple days of review are likely things we actually want rather than impulsive reactions to seeing something shiny or being in a particular mood, and if we still want them after the emotional intensity of the initial impulse has faded, they might be worth buying. This doesn't mean we should buy everything that stays in our cart, we still need to evaluate whether we can afford it and whether it aligns with our priorities, but items that survive the cooling-off period have passed one important filter that eliminates purely impulsive purchases. The cart becomes a holding area where impulses go to either dissipate or prove themselves worthy of actual purchase, and over time most impulses dissipate.

Abandoned cart emails will come from retailers trying to lure us back with discounts or free shipping or reminders about items we left behind, and we need to ignore these or unsubscribe from them rather than treating them as useful information. The emails are specifically designed to trigger fear of missing out and to make us feel like we're getting a special deal, both of which bypass rational evaluation and encourage us to complete purchases we deliberately didn't complete. If we want something enough that we'd buy it at the listed price, we can go back to our cart and buy it without needing the reminder, but responding to abandoned cart emails trains retailers to send us more of them and trains us to expect discounts for abandoning carts, which defeats the purpose of using the cart as a pause mechanism.

The cart is meant to create temporal distance between impulse and purchase, not to become a negotiation tactic with retailers, and maintaining that boundary means treating abandoned cart emails as noise rather than opportunity. We're not trying to get better deals through strategic cart abandonment, we're trying to prevent impulsive purchases that we don't actually want once the emotion fades, and that requires ignoring the emails that are designed to reignite the emotion and prompt us to complete the purchase.

Shopping lists created in advance become the authority on what we're allowed to buy, removing in-the-moment decisions that are vulnerable to impulse and marketing. We write the list when we're calm and thinking clearly, before we're in the store being bombarded with visual stimulation and sales and products we didn't come for, and we commit to buying only what's on the list and nothing else. This requires treating the list as non-negotiable, the list is boss and our in-the-moment impulses are not, which is a mental shift that takes practice but becomes easier over time. When we see something in the store that we want but that's not on the list, the answer is automatically no without needing to evaluate or justify, it's not on the list so we're not buying it, and that simplicity removes the mental negotiation that usually leads to impulse purchases.

Pre-deciding removes in-the-moment choice, and in-the-moment choice is where we're most vulnerable because we're tired from shopping and exposed to marketing and maybe hungry or stressed or rushing, all states that compromise our decision-making. The list represents our priorities as determined when we were in a good mental state, and trusting that past judgment over our current impulse usually leads to better outcomes. This works for groceries and household essentials where we can plan ahead based on what we know we need, and the discipline of sticking to the list saves significant money over time because we're not adding random items that look good in the moment but that we don't actually need.

For discretionary purchases where planning ahead is less natural, we can still create structure through rules like maintaining a wishlist that items must be on for at least two weeks before we buy them, or designating specific times when we're allowed to make discretionary purchases like the first Saturday of each month. These rules create the same temporal distance as the cart trick, forcing delay between wanting something and being able to get it, and most wants fade if we give them enough time. The rules also create scarcity around purchasing opportunities, which makes us more selective about what we choose to buy during our designated times because we know we can't just buy whatever we want whenever we want it.

Avoiding shopping when we're in vulnerable states means recognizing our patterns and choosing not to expose ourselves to temptation during times when we know we're not equipped to resist it, and this requires knowing what our vulnerable states are. If we know we buy when stressed, then being stressed is not the time to go to Target or browse Amazon or walk through the mall, we need to do something else that doesn't involve potential spending. If we know we buy when bored, then being bored is not the time to scroll through shopping apps or sale emails, we need other activities that provide stimulation without cost. If we know we buy when we're tired late at night, then evening is not the time to be on our phones with access to shopping sites.

The alternative activities need to be planned in advance because in the moment of wanting to shop we won't be able to think of alternatives, our brain will be focused on the shopping urge and won't generate other options without prompting. We need a specific list of things we can do instead: go for a walk, call a friend, watch something, exercise, read, make something, play a game, clean, cook, work on a hobby, anything that interrupts the shop-impulse pattern and gives us something else to direct our attention toward. The activities don't need to be profound or life-changing, they just need to be available and appealing enough that we'll actually do them instead of shopping when the urge hits.

Urges peak and then subside within ten to twenty minutes if we don't act on them, which means if we can distract ourselves for that long the intensity will decrease significantly and we'll be able to think more rationally about whether we actually want to shop or whether we were just responding to a temporary emotional state. This is similar to the strategy people use for food cravings or other urges, the intensity isn't constant, it rises and falls, and if we can wait out the peak the urge becomes much more manageable. Knowing this helps us commit to the alternative activity because we're not trying to resist the urge forever, just for ten or twenty minutes until it naturally decreases.

Accountability structures add external pressure that supplements our internal motivation when that motivation isn't sufficient to prevent spending we want to avoid, and this works because social pressure activates different motivational systems than self-control does. Telling someone else that we're trying to reduce spending or that we're trying not to buy specific things means we've created a social commitment that makes following through feel more important, we don't want to disappoint the person we told or have to admit we failed, and that desire to maintain social credibility adds motivation that can tip the balance when we're deciding whether to make a purchase. The accountability partner doesn't need to do anything active, just knowing they'll see our purchases or that we'll have to tell them about our spending is often enough to make us more careful.

Giving someone visibility into our checking account or credit card through shared access or through apps that allow monitoring means there are external eyes on our spending, and those eyes add a layer of consideration to purchase decisions because we're not just accountable to ourselves. Some people find this intrusive or uncomfortable, and it's important to choose an accountability partner we trust and who will approach this with support rather than judgment, someone who will ask curious questions about our purchases rather than shaming us for spending. The goal is supportive accountability that helps us stay aligned with our own stated goals, not punitive oversight that makes us feel controlled or criticized.

Accountability apps that share spending data or that require us to log purchases that we then share with someone else create technological mediation of the accountability relationship, which some people find less emotionally fraught than direct human monitoring. Apps like Honeydue or platforms that allow us to designate an accountability buddy who receives notifications about our spending create the same social pressure without requiring active involvement from the other person, they're just the audience for our behavior and their presence as audience influences our choices. The key is that we've chosen this accountability voluntarily because we recognize we need external support to maintain behavior we're struggling to maintain on our own, it's not control imposed by someone else but structure we've requested because we know it helps.

Let Something Else Remember

You meant to cancel the trial before it renewed. You meant to check the account balance before the weekend. You meant to set a reminder. The problem isn't that you don't care. The problem is that human memory wasn't built to track a dozen recurring charges across four payment methods while also running the rest of your life.

Our brain is designed for thinking and processing and making connections, not for reliably storing detailed information about recurring financial obligations that we set up months ago and haven't thought about since. Trying to remember bill due dates and subscription renewal dates and account passwords and which payment method is attached to which service is asking our working memory to do something it's not built to do, especially for people whose working memory capacity is limited by ADHD or executive function differences or just the normal constraints of human cognitive architecture. When our internal memory system can't reliably track financial details the way we need it to, we need external memory systems that hold this information for us and remind us when action is required, removing the burden from our brain and placing it on tools that don't forget or get distracted or become overwhelmed.

The calendar as a financial tool is underutilized by most people who think of calendars as being for appointments and events rather than for financial management, but calendar alerts can prevent forgotten subscriptions and missed payments and overlooked financial tasks that cost us money through late fees or unwanted charges. When we sign up for any free trial, the very first thing we do before we even use the service is set a calendar alert for the day before the trial ends with a note about what service it is and whether we want to keep it. This removes the burden of remembering trial end dates from our brain, which will not remember them, and places it on the calendar, which will remind us exactly when we need to make a decision about canceling or keeping the subscription.

Setting alerts for the day before rather than the day of gives us buffer time to actually cancel if we decide to, some cancellation processes are quick but others require phone calls during business hours or navigating through retention attempts, and having a full day means we're not rushing to cancel in the last hour before the trial ends and potentially missing the deadline. The alert should include specific information about what it's for, "cancel Peacock trial" is more useful than "trial ends" because we might have multiple trials active at once and we need to know which one this alert is about without having to try to remember or look it up.

Reminders to review subscriptions quarterly create regular checkpoints for evaluating whether we're still using and valuing the subscriptions we're paying for, because things that were valuable six months ago might not be valuable now and we won't notice that change without deliberately checking. We pick a specific recurring date, maybe the first day of each quarter or the first Monday of January, April, July, and October, something regular enough that we'll remember to do it or that we can set as a recurring calendar event. The reminder prompts us to pull our subscription list and go through each one asking whether we've used it in the last three months, whether we expect to use it in the next three months, whether the value we're getting is worth the cost, and making cancellation decisions based on honest answers to those questions.

Alerts for bill due dates even when bills are on autopay might seem redundant but serves as backup for when autopay fails, which it sometimes does because of expired credit cards or insufficient funds or technical problems on the biller's end. Getting an alert two days before a bill is due lets us verify that the autopay went through or that we have sufficient funds in the account it's drafting from, and catching problems before the due date means we can fix them without incurring late fees or service interruptions. The alerts also keep us aware of what bills are coming and when, which helps with overall financial awareness even though we're not manually paying them, we're not completely disconnected from the rhythm and cost of our recurring obligations.

Marking paydays on the calendar helps us anticipate when money will be available and when automated transfers will occur, and seeing the regular pattern of income and automated savings can be motivating because it shows the system working. Seeing that every two weeks $200 moves to savings automatically and that over a year this adds up to $5,200 makes the impact of automation visible in a way that's satisfying and that reinforces our commitment to maintaining the system. The visual representation of financial patterns helps some people's brains process financial information better than just seeing numbers in accounts, having it mapped to time creates a narrative of financial progress that's easier to understand and stay motivated by.

Phone alarms for time-sensitive financial actions create immediate interruptions that are harder to ignore than calendar notifications, which we can dismiss and then forget about. An alarm that sounds the day before a free trial ends is loud and insistent and requires us to actively engage with it, and we can set it with a label that shows on our lock screen so we know what it's for without having to unlock our phone. This works particularly well for people who struggle with following through on calendar reminders because they see them and think "I'll do that later" and then forget, alarms are harder to postpone because they're designed to be annoying enough that we deal with them immediately just to make them stop.

We can set alarms to check our bank balance before the weekend starts so we know what we have available to spend and can adjust our weekend plans if money is tighter than we thought, avoiding the situation where we overspend on Friday and Saturday and then don't have enough for something we need on Sunday or Monday. This weekly check-in becomes routine, the alarm reminds us every Friday afternoon or every Thursday evening, and over time the regular checking builds awareness of our financial status without requiring us to remember to check on our own. The alarm removes the decision about when to check and just makes it happen on schedule.

Reminders to cancel subscriptions before they renew work best when we're on the fence about keeping something and want to give it more time to prove its value but also want to make sure we don't forget to cancel if it doesn't. We're trying a subscription for the first month to see if we use it, we set an alarm for five days before it renews, the alarm goes off and prompts us to evaluate whether we've used it enough to justify another month, and we make the decision while we're being reminded rather than relying on ourselves to remember to evaluate it. This protects us from the common pattern where we mean to cancel something but the renewal happens before we get around to it and then we've paid for another month of something we decided we didn't want.

Physical notes in visible places work for people whose brains respond better to visual reminders than to digital notifications, or as supplementary reminders in addition to digital ones for really important things we absolutely cannot forget. A sticky note on our credit card that asks "do you actually need this?" gets seen every time we reach for the card, creating a moment of forced reflection before we can use it. The note doesn't prevent us from using the card if we decide we do need whatever we're buying, it just ensures we're making a conscious decision rather than using the card automatically out of habit. The physical presence of the note in our hand is harder to ignore than a digital notification we can swipe away.

A note on the bathroom mirror listing our current financial goals puts those goals in front of us every morning when we're getting ready for the day, and seeing them daily keeps them present in our mind in a way that thinking about them once and then forgetting doesn't. The goals might be "save $5000 for emergency fund," "pay off credit card," "cancel unused subscriptions," whatever we're currently working on, and seeing them regularly reinforces our commitment and makes us more likely to make choices throughout the day that align with those goals. This works because our mirror is a place we look at every single day without fail, unlike most other locations where we might put notes that we'll stop seeing after our brain habituates to them being there.

A list on the refrigerator of subscriptions we're actively paying for and why we're keeping each one makes that information visible every time we go to get food, and visibility matters because subscriptions tend to become invisible and automatic and then we forget we're paying for them. Having the list posted means we see it multiple times per day, and seeing it regularly prompts us to evaluate whether we're still getting value from each subscription, whether we've actually watched Netflix this month or whether we're paying for it out of habit. The list should include the cost of each subscription next to its name so we're confronted with the total monthly amount every time we see it, making the aggregate cost harder to ignore.

The "why we're keeping it" column is important because it forces us to articulate the value we're getting, and sometimes when we try to write down why we're keeping something we realize we don't have a good reason. If the best we can come up with is "we might use it someday" or "we used to use it a lot," that's a signal that the subscription might be ready to cancel. The act of writing and posting the list is itself a useful exercise in financial awareness, we have to gather information about all our subscriptions and think about whether each one is worth keeping, and maintaining the list means updating it when we add or cancel subscriptions, which keeps us actively aware of our subscription spending rather than letting it fade into the background.

Apps that aggregate accounts bring together all our financial information in one place so we can see our total picture without having to log in to six different bank websites and manually compile information. Mint, YNAB, Personal Capital, and similar apps connect to our bank accounts, credit cards, investment accounts, and loans through read-only access and display everything on a single dashboard with categorized spending, account balances, net worth, and upcoming bills. This centralization is valuable for people whose executive function makes it hard to remember to check multiple accounts regularly, or who find the fragmented nature of modern banking overwhelming, or who just want to reduce the friction of staying financially aware.

The apps aren't perfect, they sometimes miscategorize transactions or fail to sync with certain accounts or have interface quirks that make them frustrating to use, but even with these limitations they're generally more useful than trying to track everything manually or trying to remember to check multiple separate accounts. The aggregation means we can open one app and see whether we're on track with spending or whether we're going over in certain categories, we can see our total debt across all accounts, we can see our savings progress, we can see upcoming bills that need to be paid. The information is right there without requiring us to piece it together from multiple sources, which reduces the executive function burden and makes it more likely we'll actually look at our financial status regularly.

Some of these apps offer additional features beyond aggregation, like bill payment reminders, budget tracking, spending analysis that shows trends over time, net worth projections, investment advice, and these features can be useful if we'll actually use them, but the core value is the aggregation itself. Just having all our accounts visible in one place provides awareness that's hard to maintain when information is scattered. We should be cautious about security when giving apps access to our financial accounts, using apps from established companies with good security practices and enabling two-factor authentication wherever possible, but for many people the risk is acceptable given the benefit of having unified financial visibility.

Subscription management apps like Rocket Money, Truebill, or Hiatus specialize in identifying subscriptions and making them easy to cancel, and they're particularly valuable for people who have accumulated many subscriptions across different payment methods and platforms. These apps scan our linked accounts for recurring charges, identify which ones are subscriptions, categorize them, show us the total monthly and annual cost, and let us cancel subscriptions directly from the app without having to navigate to each service's website and deal with their deliberately confusing cancellation processes. Some services require calling to cancel or clicking through multiple retention pages, and these apps handle that friction for us, either by providing direct cancellation or by doing it on our behalf after we confirm we want to cancel.

The apps typically charge a monthly fee for their service or take a percentage of the money they save us by canceling subscriptions, and this cost is usually worth it for people who have enough forgotten or unused subscriptions that the savings significantly exceeds the app cost. Someone paying $150 per month for subscriptions they're not using can justify paying $10 per month for an app that helps them identify and cancel those subscriptions, the net saving is still $140 per month. For people with fewer subscriptions or better existing awareness of what they're paying for, the app cost might not be justified, but for those of us who know we have subscription creep problems and haven't been able to solve them manually, paying for help is a reasonable choice.

The identification feature alone is valuable even if we do the canceling ourselves, just seeing a complete list of every recurring charge across all our accounts compiled automatically gives us information we couldn't easily get otherwise. We'd have to manually review months of statements from multiple credit cards and bank accounts and payment platforms, and we'd probably still miss some subscriptions that bill quarterly or annually. The app does that work for us and presents the information clearly, and even if we choose to handle cancellations ourselves rather than paying the app to do it, having the complete inventory is worth the temporary app subscription we use for one month to do the audit and then cancel.

Virtual credit cards from services like Privacy.com or through some banks create unique card numbers for each subscription or online purchase, and these unique numbers can be paused or cancelled instantly without affecting other subscriptions or our actual credit card. This solves several problems simultaneously: it makes canceling subscriptions trivial because we just pause or delete that specific virtual card number rather than having to navigate cancellation processes, it protects our actual credit card number from being stored by multiple companies which reduces fraud risk, it gives us granular control over exactly what can charge us and when, and it makes tracking subscriptions easier because each one has its own card number with its own label.

When we sign up for a new subscription, we generate a new virtual card specifically for that subscription and label it with the service name so we know what it's for. If we decide to cancel, we just pause or delete that card number in the Privacy.com app and the subscription can't charge us anymore, no need to log in to the service or call customer service or click through retention attempts. The subscription will fail to charge, the service will probably send us emails about updating our payment information, and we can ignore those emails because we've already accomplished our goal of stopping payment. This is particularly useful for services that make cancellation deliberately difficult or for subscriptions we want to pause temporarily without fully canceling.

The virtual card approach also lets us set spending limits on specific cards, so we can give a subscription a virtual card that's limited to the exact monthly cost and if they try to charge more it will be declined. This protects against price increases that happen automatically without our approval, we'll get notified that the charge was declined and then we can decide whether the new price is worth paying or whether we want to cancel. Some subscriptions increase prices gradually hoping people won't notice, and having the card decline when the price goes up forces us to actively decide whether to continue rather than passively accepting the increase.

The physical filing system for people who work better with paper than digital, or who want paper backup for critical financial information, involves creating folders or a binder with sections for different types of financial information that needs to be accessible. One section for current subscriptions with a list of each one including the service name, cost, billing frequency, payment method, renewal date, and how to cancel. One section for bills with either paper copies if we receive them by mail or printed summaries of what we pay monthly even if the bills are paperless and on autopay. One section for account information including account numbers, website URLs, phone numbers for customer service, anything we might need if we have to call or access an account.

This system is deliberately boring and old-fashioned, but boring and functional is better than sophisticated and unused, and many people who struggle with digital organization find physical papers easier to reference and maintain. The subscription list on paper means we don't need to remember to open an app to see what we're paying for, we can flip open the binder and the information is right there. The bills section means we have a record of our recurring obligations even if everything is automatic and we never see paper bills. The account information means we're not locked out of accounts when we forget passwords or security questions, we have the information written down somewhere secure that we can access when needed.

The physical system requires maintenance, updating the subscription list when we add or cancel services, adding new bills when we take on new obligations, updating account information when we change passwords, but this maintenance is straightforward and concrete in a way that maintaining digital systems sometimes isn't. We can see the binder, we can flip through it and verify that it's current, we can add a note directly on paper without opening an app or remembering which digital system we're using. For people whose brains work better with tangible physical systems, the friction of maintaining a paper system is lower than the friction of maintaining a digital one even though digital theoretically should be easier.

Regular review schedule removes the decision about when to check our financial status by making it routine and calendar-based rather than something we do when we remember or when we feel motivated. We pick the same day each month to review accounts, maybe the first of the month or the day after payday or the last Sunday of the month, whatever date is easy to remember and that we can make into a routine. On that day we log in to all our accounts or open our aggregation app, we check balances, we verify that automated transactions happened correctly, we look at spending by category to see if anything is surprisingly high, we make sure we're not forgetting anything that needs attention.

The monthly review doesn't need to take long, fifteen or twenty minutes is usually sufficient for a basic check-in, and having it scheduled means we're not relying on remembering to do it or feeling motivated to do it, it's just the thing we do on that day. Over time this builds financial awareness without requiring constant attention, we're checking in regularly enough to catch problems early but not so frequently that it becomes burdensome. Some people need more frequent review if their financial situation is particularly tight or if they're actively working on reducing spending, and weekly reviews work better for them, but monthly is a good baseline for maintenance once we have systems established.

The same day each quarter for subscription audit gives us regular opportunity to cancel things we've stopped using before we've paid for too many additional months, subscriptions we were using in January might not be valuable by April, and quarterly review catches those changes before we've wasted six or nine months of payments. This is different from the monthly review, we're not just checking that subscriptions are billing correctly, we're evaluating whether we want to keep them at all based on recent usage. The quarterly timing is frequent enough that we're not paying for unused subscriptions for extended periods, but not so frequent that we're constantly evaluating and potentially canceling things we just haven't used in the past few weeks but will use again soon.

The same day each year for comprehensive financial review is for bigger-picture assessment that doesn't make sense to do monthly or quarterly, looking at our overall financial progress, evaluating whether our systems are still working or need adjustment, thinking about larger goals and whether we're making progress toward them. This might involve looking at annual spending across all categories, net worth change over the past year, progress on debt payoff or savings goals, evaluation of whether we need to adjust automated amounts based on income or expense changes. The annual review is a zoom-out moment where we're looking at patterns and trends rather than individual transactions or monthly fluctuations.

Annual review also catches subscriptions or expenses that bill annually rather than monthly, these are particularly easy to forget because they don't show up in our regular monthly review and they might not be caught by subscription identification apps if they haven't billed recently. Annual bills for domain names or website hosting or software licenses or membership organizations can surprise us if we're not expecting them, and having a designated time each year to look for them means we can anticipate the charges and decide whether to renew or cancel before they auto-renew.

Why external memory works is that our brain is fundamentally better at processing and thinking than at storing detailed factual information, and asking it to do both simultaneously means neither function works as well as it could. When we offload storage to external systems that are designed for reliable information retention, we free our brain to focus on processing and decision-making, which is what it's actually good at. We can think about whether a subscription is valuable instead of trying to remember that we have the subscription in the first place. We can evaluate purchase decisions instead of trying to remember what our account balance is. We can plan for upcoming expenses instead of trying to remember when bills are due.

For people with executive function challenges this separation is even more critical because working memory limitations mean we have less capacity for holding information even temporarily, and asking our brain to both remember financial details and process financial decisions at the same time is asking too much. External memory systems compensate for working memory limitations by holding the details externally where they're always accessible, and this compensation is what makes financial management possible for people who can't rely on their internal memory to track everything that needs tracking. The systems aren't a crutch or a sign of weakness, they're appropriate tools for matching our capabilities to the task requirements, using external storage for storage tasks so our brain can focus on cognitive tasks.

The Real Reason We're Buying

You got some bad news at work. By the time you got home you'd already bought three things you don't remember choosing. Nothing you actually wanted. Nothing you needed. Just the particular relief that comes from clicking purchase when everything else feels like it's slipping.

We buy things when we're sad or stressed or bored not because we need the things we're buying but because the process of buying provides temporary relief from negative emotions, and understanding this distinction matters because it means we're not actually addressing the underlying feeling, we're just medicating it briefly with dopamine before it comes back stronger and often accompanied by guilt about the money we spent. Shopping as emotional regulation works in the moment because it genuinely does provide neurochemical relief, the dopamine spike from anticipating and acquiring something counteracts sadness and anxiety and boredom in ways that feel significant while they're happening, but the relief is short-lived and the original emotion returns as soon as the dopamine fades, usually within twenty minutes to an hour, leaving us back where we started except now we're also dealing with buyer's remorse or financial stress or the physical presence of things we don't actually want.

The types of emotional spending have different triggers but similar mechanisms, we're using shopping to regulate our internal state rather than to acquire things we need. Stress shopping happens when we're overwhelmed by work or relationships or life circumstances and our brain is desperately seeking anything that will provide relief from the constant activation of our stress response, shopping offers temporary escape from thinking about our problems and temporary elevation of mood through anticipation and acquisition, but it doesn't reduce the actual stressors and often adds financial stress to the existing pile. Boredom shopping happens when we're understimulated and our brain is seeking something interesting or engaging to focus on, scrolling through products and reading descriptions and imagining how we'd use things provides stimulation that feels better than the flat empty feeling of boredom, but it's a expensive way to address understimulation when going for a walk or calling someone or doing something creative would work just as well without costing money.

Celebration shopping happens when something good occurs and we want to mark the occasion or reward ourselves, our brain associates positive events with treats and shopping is an easily accessible treat that feels appropriate as a way to acknowledge achievements. The problem is that we end up spending money that could go toward whatever we're celebrating or toward other financial goals, and the purchase often has nothing to do with what we're celebrating, we're just using the positive emotion as permission to buy something we've been wanting or to browse without our usual restraint. Sadness shopping provides temporary comfort when we're feeling down, buying something new gives us something to look forward to when life feels difficult, and the brief period of excitement about a purchase can interrupt a cycle of rumination or negative thinking, but the sadness returns unchanged by the purchase and we've added an object we don't need and probably guilt about spending money we shouldn't have.

Angry shopping works as rebellion or assertion of autonomy, we're angry about something in our life and buying things feels like taking control or doing what we want regardless of consequences or treating ourselves when we feel like external circumstances are treating us poorly. The purchases are often impulsive and motivated by "I deserve this" thinking that's coming from anger rather than actual desire for the item, and once the anger fades we're left with purchases that don't make sense and that we might not have made in a neutral emotional state. Anxious shopping attempts to feel prepared for future scenarios our anxiety is catastrophizing about, if we're worried about potential problems we buy things that would theoretically help us handle those problems if they occurred, which gives us a false sense of control over uncertain futures and temporarily quiets the anxiety about not being prepared enough.

"Retail therapy" as a term acknowledges that shopping serves a therapeutic function for many people, that it genuinely makes us feel better temporarily, and that temporary better is valuable when we're struggling. The concept isn't wrong, shopping does provide mood regulation through neurochemical processes that are real and measurable, the problem is that it's an unsustainable coping mechanism that creates additional problems while temporarily masking the original ones. It works in the moment because our brain gets dopamine and our attention gets redirected away from negative emotions and we have something tangible to show for our effort, but it fails long-term because the emotional relief doesn't last and the financial consequences compound and we haven't developed more sustainable ways to manage difficult feelings.

The financial stress created by emotional spending often becomes its own trigger for more emotional spending, creating a vicious cycle where we feel bad about money so we shop to feel better which makes our money situation worse which makes us feel worse which drives more shopping. Breaking this cycle requires recognizing that shopping is temporarily effective emotional regulation and that we need to find replacement coping mechanisms that provide similar relief without the financial cost, not just telling ourselves to stop shopping and expecting that to work when shopping is meeting a genuine need for mood management even if it's doing so in a problematic way.

Recognizing the pattern starts with noticing when we're shopping because we feel something rather than because we need something, and this distinction isn't always obvious in the moment because our brain is very good at generating justifications for why we need whatever we're buying. If we're shopping because we feel stressed and we need something to help us relax, we'll convince ourselves that we need new pajamas or a particular book or some item that will enable relaxation, when actually we're just stressed and looking for any purchase that will provide temporary relief. If we're shopping because we're bored and want stimulation, we'll convince ourselves that we need a new hobby supply or gadget or organizational system, when actually we're just bored and shopping is providing the stimulation we're seeking regardless of what we buy.

The test is whether we were thinking about needing this item before the emotional state hit, if we've been planning to buy new pajamas for weeks because our current ones are falling apart then buying them now is addressing a real need, but if the idea of needing pajamas occurred to us after we started feeling stressed then we're probably shopping to manage stress rather than to solve a pajama problem. Paying attention to the sequence matters, emotional state followed by sudden awareness of a need is usually emotional shopping, awareness of a need followed by planning when to address it is usually practical shopping. This isn't a perfect test because sometimes we do genuinely need things and we remember that need when we're emotional, but it's a useful heuristic for catching most emotional purchases.

If we're shopping because we feel something rather than because we need something, the item won't fix the feeling, and understanding this cognitively doesn't stop us from hoping it will in the moment. When we're sad and we see something that sparks joy, we imagine that owning that thing will maintain the spark of joy and improve our overall mood, and that imagination is compelling enough that we buy it even though we know intellectually that objects don't work that way. By the time the package arrives the sadness has usually passed on its own or morphed into different feelings, and the item that seemed so important when we ordered it is now just another thing we own that doesn't do anything to address our emotional landscape. The feeling and the item were never actually connected, we created a false connection in our mind because we were seeking relief and shopping was available.

What to do instead requires having alternate coping strategies planned in advance because in the moment of feeling bad our brain will default to whatever has worked before, and if shopping has worked before then that's where our attention will go automatically. We need to have other options that are immediately accessible and that provide some of the same benefits shopping provides, whether that's distraction or stimulation or a sense of control or temporary mood elevation. Going for a walk provides distraction and often helps with stress and sad moods through physical movement and change of environment, and it's free and immediately available in most situations. Calling a friend provides social connection and distraction and sometimes perspective on whatever we're feeling, and if we're feeling isolated or lonely it addresses that directly rather than trying to shop our way to feeling less alone.

Exercising provides both dopamine release and distraction, the physical exertion activates our reward system in ways that are similar to shopping but without the financial cost and with actual health benefits rather than accumulated objects. Making something creative provides engagement and stimulation and a sense of accomplishment, whether that's cooking or drawing or building or writing or any activity where we're actively producing rather than passively consuming, and the engagement interrupts negative emotional states by giving us something concrete to focus on. These alternatives need to be written down in a list we can reference when we're feeling the urge to shop, because remembering them in the moment is hard when our brain is focused on the shopping urge and generating justifications for why we should buy something.

The list should include specific activities rather than general categories, "go for a walk around the block" is more actionable than "exercise" because it removes the decision-making about what kind of exercise and how long and where. "Call Sarah" is more actionable than "call a friend" because we're not making the additional decision about which friend to call when we're already feeling emotionally depleted. The more specific and concrete the alternatives are, the more likely we are to actually do them instead of defaulting to shopping, and we should include things at different energy levels because sometimes we're capable of going for a run and sometimes we can barely get off the couch, and both states need alternatives that are appropriately matched to our available energy.

The urge surfing technique borrowed from addiction treatment and applied to spending urges involves recognizing that urges have a natural arc, they rise in intensity and then peak and then subside if we don't act on them, and the whole cycle typically takes ten to twenty minutes. When the urge to buy something hits, instead of immediately acting on it or trying to suppress it, we acknowledge it and commit to waiting ten minutes doing something else before we make any decision about whether to buy. We set a timer for ten minutes and do one of the alternative activities from our list, and usually by the time the timer goes off the urge has decreased enough that we can think more rationally about whether we actually want to make the purchase.

Urges feel unbearable in the moment because they're at peak intensity and our brain is telling us we need to act right now, but if we can tolerate the discomfort for just a few minutes the intensity naturally decreases regardless of whether we act on the urge. This is the same principle people use for cravings for food or cigarettes or any other thing they're trying to resist, the biological mechanism is the same, an urge peaks and subsides and we can ride that wave instead of responding to it immediately. Knowing this intellectually helps us commit to the ten-minute wait because we're not trying to resist forever, just until the peak passes and the urge becomes manageable enough that our rational brain can engage with whether we actually want what we're thinking about buying.

The surfing metaphor is useful because it implies active engagement rather than passive suffering, we're not just white-knuckling through the urge, we're riding it like a wave that we know will crest and fall. During the ten minutes we're actively doing something else, engaging with an alternative activity, not just sitting there staring at the clock and suffering, and the active engagement helps the time pass and provides competing stimulation that reduces the intensity of the shopping urge. Sometimes after the ten minutes we decide we do still want to make the purchase and it's not purely emotional, and that's fine, the goal isn't to never buy anything, it's to create space between urge and action so we're making conscious choices rather than acting on emotional impulse.

When professional help is needed isn't always obvious because the line between "I shop more than I'd like" and "my shopping is compulsive and causing serious harm" isn't sharp, but there are signs that self-help strategies aren't sufficient and that working with a therapist would be valuable. If spending is compulsive to the point where we feel unable to stop even when we want to, where we're buying things we don't want or need and experiencing significant distress about it but continuing to do it anyway, that suggests a level of compulsivity that needs professional intervention. If we're hiding spending from partners or family members, lying about purchases or hiding packages or having secret credit cards, that level of secrecy indicates shame that's significant enough that we need support in addressing both the spending and the underlying issues the secrecy is trying to conceal.

If we're in debt specifically from impulse buying and the debt is serious enough to threaten our financial stability or future but we can't stop adding to it, that's a sign that the behavior has progressed beyond what we can manage on our own with better systems. If we've tried multiple approaches to reducing spending and nothing has worked for more than a few weeks, if we keep returning to the same patterns despite genuine desire to change, professional help can provide insights and strategies we haven't been able to access on our own. If the shopping is connected to other mental health struggles like depression or anxiety or trauma, addressing those underlying issues with professional support will often reduce the emotional shopping as a secondary effect because we're no longer using shopping as our primary coping mechanism for difficult feelings.

Therapy for compulsive shopping or spending problems can take several forms, cognitive behavioral therapy helps us identify the thoughts and beliefs that trigger spending and develop alternative responses, dialectical behavior therapy teaches distress tolerance and emotion regulation skills that reduce the need for shopping as emotional management, and some therapists specialize in financial therapy or money disorders specifically. The goal isn't to never spend money or to eliminate all emotional connection to purchasing, it's to develop a healthier relationship with spending where we're in control rather than feeling controlled by urges we can't resist, where we can buy things we want and value without the compulsive quality that makes spending feel out of our control.

Building a healthier relationship with money involves recognizing several truths that run counter to consumer culture messaging but that are necessary for breaking the cycle of using shopping to manage emotions. Things can't make us happy in any lasting way, material possessions provide temporary satisfaction that fades quickly once we own them, and pursuing happiness through acquisition is fundamentally doomed because happiness doesn't come from having things, it comes from entirely different sources like relationships and purpose and growth and contribution. This doesn't mean we can't enjoy things or that buying things is wrong, it means we need to have realistic expectations about what things can do for us, which is provide utility or convenience or beauty or pleasure but not fundamental life satisfaction or emotional wellbeing.

The temporary satisfaction that new purchases provide is real but it's temporary, acknowledging both parts of that is important. The first day or week of owning something new feels good, we're excited about it and we use it frequently and we feel pleased that we have it, but that novelty wears off quickly and the item becomes just another thing we own that we mostly don't think about. Consumer culture tells us the solution is to buy more new things to recreate that novelty feeling, and we can do that, but it's expensive and unsustainable and it doesn't lead anywhere except to more buying. Recognizing that the novelty will wear off and that's normal helps us make more intentional choices about whether we want to spend money to get a few days or weeks of satisfaction, sometimes that's worth it and sometimes it's not, but we're making the choice consciously rather than expecting the satisfaction to last indefinitely and being disappointed when it doesn't.

Separating our worth from our stuff means recognizing that we're not what we own, our value as people isn't demonstrated by having the right brands or the newest products or a home that looks like it came from a magazine. Consumer culture constantly reinforces the opposite message, that we should judge ourselves and others by what we own, that having nice things means we're successful or sophisticated or tasteful, that not having those things means we're failing in some way. This is messaging designed to make us spend money, it's not truth about human value, but it's so pervasive that we internalize it without realizing we're doing it. When we notice ourselves thinking "I need this to be the kind of person I want to be" or "people will think I'm successful if I have this" or "I'll feel better about myself if I own this," we're confusing identity with possessions in ways that drive spending that doesn't actually serve us.

Finding other sources of dopamine that don't cost money becomes important once we recognize that we're using shopping primarily for the neurochemical hit rather than for the items themselves, and this means identifying activities that activate our reward system without requiring spending. Physical activity releases dopamine and endorphins, spending time with people we care about activates reward and bonding neurochemicals, accomplishing tasks or making progress on goals provides satisfaction, learning new things engages our curiosity and reward systems, creating things activates multiple reward pathways. These alternatives aren't perfect substitutes for shopping, they require more effort and they don't work instantly the way buying something does, but they're sustainable in ways that shopping isn't and they often provide more lasting satisfaction even though the initial activation takes longer.

Building a repertoire of free or low-cost dopamine sources takes intentional effort because shopping has become our default, it's what we turn to automatically when we want to feel better, and developing new defaults requires repeatedly choosing alternatives until they become automatic. This is hard, it's genuinely hard to choose going for a walk when we could buy something that would make us feel better right now, but the more we practice the alternatives the easier they become and the less powerful the shopping urge becomes over time. We're essentially retraining our brain about where to seek reward when we're stressed or bored or sad, shifting from external acquisition to internal or relational or embodied sources of satisfaction, and that retraining takes time and repetition but eventually leads to patterns that are more sustainable financially and often more satisfying emotionally than shopping ever was.

You Are Not Your Spending

Somewhere along the way, being bad with money stopped being a description of your behavior and became a description of you. It's easier to believe it's who you are than to keep trying systems that don't seem to work. But the belief itself is part of what's keeping you stuck.

How we think about ourselves in relation to money shapes our behavior more than we usually recognize, and when we've internalized the belief that we're "just bad with money" that belief becomes self-fulfilling because it removes our sense of agency about changing our patterns. Saying "I'm bad with money" frames spending problems as intrinsic personality traits rather than as behaviors that can be modified with appropriate systems, and this framing makes us passive observers of our own financial disaster rather than active participants who can build different infrastructure. The identity of being bad with money becomes comfortable in a perverse way because it explains our struggles and removes the expectation that we should be able to do better, but it also traps us in those struggles because we're not trying to change something we believe is fundamental to who we are.

Money and self-worth get tangled together through messages we've absorbed from childhood about what financial success means about our character, our intelligence, our capability as adults. Being "good with money" is treated as a moral virtue that reflects discipline and responsibility and forward-thinking maturity, while being "bad with money" is treated as a moral failing that reflects impulsiveness and irresponsibility and inability to manage adult life. These aren't neutral assessments of financial skills, they're judgments about our worth as people, and we internalize them in ways that make financial struggles feel like evidence that we're fundamentally deficient rather than evidence that we need different tools. When we overspend or carry debt or don't have savings, we experience that as shameful proof that we're failing at being a functional adult rather than as information about where our current systems aren't working.

The shame prevents us from asking for help or learning strategies because admitting we need help means admitting we can't handle something we think we should just know how to do, and exposing our financial struggles to others feels like exposing our fundamental inadequacy. We hide our debt, we don't talk about how much we're spending, we pretend we have things figured out even when we're drowning, and the hiding means we're trying to solve these problems alone without access to other people's knowledge or experience or support. The shame is part of what keeps us stuck, we can't fix problems we're too ashamed to acknowledge, and we can't learn strategies we're too ashamed to admit we need.

Reframing this from moral failure to practical challenge requires actively rejecting the narrative that financial struggles mean something about our character, and this rejection has to be repeated because the cultural messages are constant and pervasive. When we notice ourselves thinking "I'm such a failure with money" or "I should be better at this," we need to interrupt that thought and replace it with something more accurate like "I have a brain that works differently with money and I need different systems" or "I haven't had the right tools yet but I can build systems that work for me." This isn't just positive thinking, it's accurate thinking that focuses on behavior and systems rather than identity and character, and that focus on changeable factors rather than fixed traits is what makes improvement possible.

The comparison trap operates constantly in our culture where we're exposed to other people's possessions and lifestyles through social media and advertising and just seeing what people around us have, and our brain automatically uses that information to evaluate whether we're doing okay or falling behind. Seeing what other people have triggers thoughts like "they have their finances figured out and I don't" or "they can afford nice things and I'm struggling to pay bills" or "everyone else is successful and I'm failing," and these comparisons make us feel inadequate in ways that often trigger more spending as we try to close the perceived gap between where we are and where we think we should be based on what we see others having.

What we don't see is that many people who appear financially successful are actually drowning in debt, that the beautiful home and nice cars and frequent vacations are often financed by credit cards and loans that are creating immense stress beneath the surface that appears successful. We're comparing our behind-the-scenes financial reality to other people's curated public presentation, and this comparison is inherently distorted because we know all our own struggles and mistakes while we only see the polished exterior that others choose to show. Some people genuinely do have their finances figured out and have no debt and significant savings, and that's real, but many more people are presenting an image of financial success while privately struggling with the same issues we are, and we have no way to tell the difference from the outside.

Social media intensifies this comparison because it's specifically designed to show highlight reels and aspirational content rather than mundane reality, we see people's best purchases and nicest possessions and most impressive experiences, and we don't see the debt or the stress or the financial trade-offs that made those things possible. The people posting about their new car aren't posting about the $600 monthly payment or the fact that they're now house-poor because of the car payment, the people posting vacation photos aren't posting about the credit card debt the vacation created or about the fact that they can't afford to go out to eat for the next three months. We see the acquisition and the experience without seeing the financial context, and our brain assumes that if they can afford these things their overall financial situation must be solid, when actually we have no information about their finances beyond what they choose to show.

Unfollowing or muting people whose lifestyles trigger comparison and inadequacy is self-protection, not judgment, we're recognizing that exposure to certain content makes us feel worse about our own situation and makes us want to spend money trying to replicate what we're seeing. This doesn't mean those people are doing anything wrong, it means we're vulnerable to comparison in ways that aren't serving us, and we need to protect ourselves by reducing exposure to triggers. Some people can follow aspirational content without it affecting their spending, their brains don't make the same connections between seeing and wanting that ours do, and that's fine for them. For us, if seeing certain content consistently makes us feel inadequate or triggers shopping, we need to stop seeing that content regardless of whether it's reasonable that it affects us that way.

Consumption as identity means we're using the things we own to communicate who we are or who we want to be, and consumer culture encourages this conflation of identity with possessions because it makes us keep buying things as we try to construct and maintain the self we want to present to the world. We buy certain brands to signal that we're the kind of person who values quality or sustainability or status, we buy certain types of products to show that we're into fitness or cooking or technology or whatever identity we're cultivating, and the buying becomes part of how we understand ourselves rather than just a means of acquiring things we need. This means we're constantly buying things not because we need them functionally but because they represent the kind of person we think we are or want to be, and this representation through objects is expensive and endless because there's always something else that could signal our identity more clearly or more impressively.

The stuff we own becomes shorthand for personality, we look around our homes and see our purchases as reflections of who we are, the books we'll read someday represent us as intellectual, the exercise equipment represents us as fit or at least fitness-oriented, the craft supplies represent us as creative, the kitchen gadgets represent us as someone who cooks elaborate meals. The problem is that we're often buying representations of aspirational selves rather than supporting actual behaviors, we buy the exercise equipment but we don't actually work out regularly, we buy the craft supplies but we don't actually make things, we buy the kitchen gadgets but we still eat takeout most nights. The objects represent an identity we'd like to have but aren't actually living, and they accumulate as evidence of the gap between who we want to be and who we are, which often triggers shame that leads to more aspirational purchases in a cycle that doesn't resolve the underlying gap.

Buying things to represent aspirational identity is particularly expensive because it's not limited by actual need, we can always buy more things that represent the person we want to be because the person we want to be is an ideal that's always slightly out of reach. The person who wants to be athletic can always buy more workout clothes or equipment or supplements, the person who wants to be intellectual can always buy more books, the person who wants to be creative can always buy more supplies for new hobbies they haven't tried yet. The buying is motivated by the hope that having the right things will transform us into the person we want to be, that if we have all the equipment we'll suddenly start working out consistently or that if we have all the craft supplies we'll suddenly become prolific makers, but objects don't create behavior change, and we're left with expensive representations of selves we're not actually inhabiting.

The deprivation mindset is what happens when we frame any spending limits as loss or restriction, "I can't buy anything" or "I can't have nice things" or "I have to deprive myself," and this framing creates psychological rebellion where we feel punished and deprived and eventually break the restrictions with compensatory overspending. Restriction and binge cycles with money work the same way they do with food, when we're restricting we feel deprived and we build up resentment about the restrictions, and eventually that pressure breaks and we binge-spend as compensation for the period of deprivation, buying multiple things we've been wanting and telling ourselves we deserve them after being so careful. Then we feel guilty about the binge and reimpose strict restrictions, and the cycle repeats.

Framing financial management as deprivation guarantees this cycle because no one can maintain feelings of deprivation indefinitely, we're psychologically wired to resist and rebel against deprivation, and any system built on ongoing deprivation will eventually collapse as we compensate for what we feel we've been denied. The solution isn't trying harder to maintain deprivation or feeling more guilty about breaking restrictions, it's reframing the entire approach so it's not about deprivation at all but about choice and intentionality. We're not depriving ourselves of things, we're choosing to spend money on what matters most to us rather than spending it thoughtlessly on everything, and that reframe from deprivation to choice changes the emotional experience significantly.

"I can't buy this" triggers deprivation and resistance, "I'm choosing not to buy this so I can spend money on things I care more about" frames the same action as agency and priority-setting rather than restriction imposed from outside. The actual behavior is the same, we're not buying the thing either way, but the psychological experience is completely different because in one frame we're being denied something we want and in the other frame we're making a choice that aligns with our values and goals. Developing the habit of framing things as choice rather than restriction takes practice because the deprivation frame is our default, but the practice pays off in sustainability because we can maintain choices much longer than we can maintain feelings of deprivation.

Reframing financial management as intentionality rather than deprivation means focusing on choosing what matters enough to spend on rather than on restricting ourselves from everything, and this requires actually thinking about what we value and want our money to support. We can't just decide "I'm going to be more intentional with money" without defining what intentional means for us specifically, we need to identify what we care about enough to prioritize financially. Maybe travel is important to us and worth spending money on while fancy coffee every day isn't, maybe having a nice home environment is worth it while having the latest phone isn't, maybe experiences with people we care about are worth it while material possessions mostly aren't. The specifics matter less than the process of consciously deciding what's worth spending on rather than defaulting to spending on everything that crosses our path.

Building financial goals that actually motivate requires making them concrete and visual rather than vague and abstract, because our brains respond to concrete specific goals much more strongly than to general ones. "Save money" doesn't motivate behavior change because it's too abstract, we don't know how much or by when or for what purpose, and abstract goals don't activate the reward systems that make working toward them feel satisfying. "Save five thousand dollars by December for six-week trip to Japan" is concrete and specific and creates clear motivation because we can visualize what we're working toward, we can picture the trip and imagine being there and connect current actions like not buying random stuff to that future experience we want to have.

The specificity makes the goal feel real rather than theoretical, we're saving for something concrete that we can describe and research and plan rather than saving for the vague concept of financial security that never feels close enough to be rewarding. Visual reminders of what we're working toward help maintain motivation when the goal is months or years away, putting a picture of our goal destination on our mirror or phone background or refrigerator means we're reminded of what we're choosing every time we might be tempted to spend money on something less important to us. The reminder connects immediate actions to future outcomes in ways that help us make choices aligned with what we actually want, not spending on this random thing now means being closer to the thing we really want later.

Connecting current actions to future outcomes we care about is something our brain struggles with naturally because of temporal discounting, we heavily weight immediate rewards and heavily discount future ones, which is why it's so hard to save for the future when spending provides immediate satisfaction. Visual reminders and concrete goals partially overcome this tendency by making the future feel more present and real, when we can vividly imagine the trip we're saving for or the debt freedom we're working toward or the emergency fund that will reduce our financial stress, those future outcomes become more motivating than they would be if they were just abstract concepts. This doesn't completely override our preference for immediate gratification, but it provides enough counter-motivation that we can sometimes choose the future goal over the immediate purchase.

The "enough" problem is that consumer culture makes enough feel impossible, there's always something newer or better or more, and we're constantly exposed to messages that what we have isn't sufficient and we need upgrades or additions or replacements. Advertising exists specifically to make us feel that what we have isn't enough and that we need what they're selling to be complete or satisfied or successful, and this constant messaging creates perpetual dissatisfaction with what we own and perpetual desire for more. Learning to recognize when we actually have enough requires actively rejecting consumer culture's definition of enough and developing our own standards based on what actually serves our lives rather than what we're told we should have.

Enough means our needs are met and our important wants are satisfied, and beyond that point additional stuff doesn't improve our lives proportionally to its cost. We need shelter and food and clothing and transportation, and beyond meeting those needs we might want comfort or convenience or beauty or particular capabilities that make our lives better in ways we value. Those wants are legitimate, and having enough includes satisfying wants that actually matter to us, but not every want is equally important and not everything we think we want will actually improve our lives if we get it. Developing the ability to distinguish between wants that will genuinely enhance our life and wants that are manufactured by advertising or social comparison or aspirational identity takes practice and honesty with ourselves.

Asking "do I actually have enough of this category of thing" before buying more helps identify when we're buying beyond the point of utility, we probably don't need a twentieth mug when we have nineteen that work fine, we probably don't need another black shirt when we have ten in our closet, we probably don't need more kitchen gadgets when we're not using the ones we have. Having enough doesn't mean having exactly one of everything, it means having sufficient quantity and quality to meet our needs and wants without excess that creates clutter and financial drain. Some people need more of certain things than others based on their life circumstances and preferences, someone who works from home and drinks coffee all day might legitimately need more mugs than someone who drinks one coffee per day at a coffee shop, and that's fine, enough is personal not universal.

The practice of checking whether we have enough before buying more gradually builds awareness of our existing possessions in ways that reduce impulse buying, when we're in the habit of thinking "do I have enough of this already" before purchasing we're less likely to buy duplicates or unnecessary additions. This practice works best when we've actually assessed what we own rather than guessing, going through closets and cabinets and seeing what we have shows us patterns we weren't aware of, like that we apparently buy black shirts repeatedly or that we have five unopened things of the same product because we kept forgetting we had it. The awareness of what we already own reduces purchases motivated by forgetting what we have or by thinking we need something we actually already possess.

Changing the narrative from "I'm bad with money" to "I have a brain that works differently with money and I need different systems" removes moral judgment and focuses on practical solutions, and this reframe is important enough that it deserves repetition even though we've touched on it already. We're not bad people or deficient adults, we have brains with particular characteristics that make certain financial tasks harder than they are for people whose brains work differently. Working memory limitations, executive function differences, impulse control challenges, heightened sensitivity to dopamine-seeking behaviors, these are neurological realities that affect how we interact with money and spending, and they're not character flaws any more than needing glasses is a character flaw.

People whose brains make working memory and planning and sustained attention easy don't have superior character, they just have cognitive profiles that happen to align well with what standard financial management requires. Those of us whose brains work differently need different approaches that account for our cognitive profiles rather than fighting against them, and that's a reasonable accommodation not a moral compromise. When we stop treating spending problems as evidence that we're bad people and start treating them as information about what kind of systems we need to build, we can actually address them instead of just feeling ashamed and stuck. The shame doesn't help, it just keeps us from doing anything about the situation because we're too busy feeling terrible about ourselves to build functional infrastructure.

We're not trying to become people who naturally track every dollar or who can resist any impulse or who find budgeting satisfying and intuitive, we're trying to build systems that work for us as we actually are. This means automation for things our brain won't remember, physical barriers for impulses we can't reliably resist, external memory for information we can't hold internally, structure that removes decisions we're not equipped to make well repeatedly. The goal is functionality not transformation, having systems that let us meet our financial obligations and save something and not constantly overspend, not becoming fundamentally different people with different brains. We're working with our brains as they are and building around our limitations rather than pretending those limitations don't exist or that we should be able to overcome them through effort alone.

The System Is the Point

You don't need to become a different person. You need different infrastructure. That's the whole argument — and it's a more hopeful one than it might sound.

Standard financial advice assumes everyone's brain works the same way and that money management is fundamentally a matter of trying harder, having more discipline, caring more about our financial future, and when we can't make that advice work we conclude that we're the problem rather than recognizing that the advice is built for cognitive profiles different from ours. The budget apps and tracking spreadsheets and advice to just stop buying things we don't need all assume that knowing what to do equals being able to do it consistently, that having information is the same as having capability, and for people whose brains work a certain way that assumption is accurate and the standard advice is sufficient. For those of us whose brains work differently, whose working memory doesn't reliably hold financial details, whose impulse control is compromised under stress, whose executive function makes planning and sustained attention difficult, the standard advice feels impossible to follow and the failure to follow it feels like personal inadequacy rather than like a mismatch between our cognitive reality and the tools we've been given.

We're not failures and we're not stupid. We're capable intelligent people who happen to have brains that need different infrastructure for financial management than what standard advice provides, and there's no moral dimension to this, it's just a practical reality about cognitive diversity and how different brains need different supports to accomplish the same tasks. Someone who needs glasses isn't morally inferior to someone with naturally perfect vision, they just need tools to compensate for how their eyes work, and someone who needs external memory systems and automation and physical barriers to spending isn't morally inferior to someone who can track everything mentally and resist impulses through willpower alone, they just need different tools to compensate for how their brain works.

The struggles we have with remembering subscriptions and resisting impulses and making decisions when tired and tracking spending and all the other challenges we've discussed throughout this book are real struggles, they're not excuses or laziness or not trying hard enough. They're the predictable results of trying to use systems designed for different brains, and the solution isn't to keep trying harder at approaches that fundamentally don't match our cognitive capabilities, it's to build different systems that work with our brains as they actually are rather than as financial advice assumes they should be. This isn't giving up or accepting defeat, it's recognizing reality and responding to it appropriately instead of continuing to beat ourselves up for not being able to make inadequate tools work through sheer force of will.

The systems that work are the ones that account for how our brains actually operate: automation instead of relying on willpower that depletes under stress, external memory instead of trying to remember everything internally when our working memory can't hold that much information, physical barriers that add friction to spending instead of trying to resist frictionless purchasing through self-control we don't consistently have. These systems remove the need for abilities we struggle with, the automation remembers when our memory doesn't, the barriers interrupt impulses when our impulse control fails, the external tracking holds information our brain can't hold reliably. This isn't accommodation in the sense of lowering standards, it's accommodation in the sense of providing appropriate tools that let us achieve the same outcomes through different methods.

None of these systems require us to become different people or to develop capabilities we don't have, they work precisely because they're designed around our limitations rather than requiring us to overcome those limitations through effort. We don't have to become naturally organized or naturally good at tracking details or naturally able to resist every temptation, we just have to set up systems once when we're thinking clearly and then let those systems do the ongoing work of managing our finances. The initial setup takes effort and attention, but once the systems are in place they run with minimal ongoing input from us, and that's exactly what we need because ongoing effort and attention are what we don't have in sustainable quantities.

The goal isn't becoming someone who never wants to buy things or who naturally tracks every dollar or who can resist any impulse or who finds financial planning intuitive and satisfying. Those capabilities would be nice but they're not necessary, and striving for them sets us up for failure because we're trying to change fundamental aspects of how our brain works rather than building around those aspects. The actual achievable goal is having enough money left at the end of the month to pay bills and save something, not constantly overspending and wondering where everything went, being aware of our subscriptions and canceling ones we don't use, making conscious spending decisions at least some of the time rather than operating on pure impulse. These are modest goals in some ways, they're not financial independence or early retirement or perfect optimization, but for those of us who have been struggling they represent significant meaningful improvement in daily financial stress and long-term financial trajectory.

Money shame is pervasive in our culture and entirely unhelpful for actually changing behavior, we've been taught explicitly and implicitly that struggling with money means we're irresponsible or immature or lacking in basic adult competencies, and we've internalized these messages in ways that make every financial mistake feel like confirmation that we're deficient. The shame doesn't motivate us to do better, it just makes us feel worse and often triggers more spending as we try to cope with feeling bad about ourselves, creating cycles where shame leads to spending leads to more shame. Understanding the neuroscience and psychology behind why we spend the way we do doesn't excuse the behavior or eliminate responsibility for it, but it does remove the moral judgment and the shame by showing that these patterns are rooted in how our brains work rather than in character flaws or personal failures.

We can acknowledge that impulse buying is happening because of dopamine systems and still take responsibility for building barriers that interrupt those impulses before we act on them. We can understand that decision fatigue is real and depleting and still structure our lives to avoid shopping when we're tired. We can recognize that working memory limitations make subscription tracking genuinely hard and still set up external systems that track them for us. The neuroscience explains the difficulty without removing our agency to address it, and that balance between understanding and action is what makes change possible without requiring us to become different people or to somehow develop cognitive capabilities we don't have.

The choice we're facing is between continuing to try the same strategies that haven't worked while feeling increasingly terrible about ourselves, or acknowledging that we need different systems and building those systems without shame about needing them. The first option is familiar and in some ways easier because it doesn't require us to admit that standard advice doesn't work for us, we can keep blaming ourselves for not executing it properly rather than questioning whether the advice itself is the problem. But familiarity and ease don't make this option effective, we know from experience that trying harder at the same approaches leads to the same results, and choosing to keep doing that is choosing to stay stuck. The second option requires accepting that we're not going to become naturally good at financial management through willpower and effort, that our brain works differently and will continue to work differently, and that we need to build external structure that compensates for this rather than fighting against it.

Accepting that we need different systems isn't giving up or admitting defeat, it's recognizing reality and choosing to respond to it effectively rather than continuing to pretend our brain works differently than it does. There's no virtue in struggling with inadequate tools when appropriate tools are available, and there's no shame in using automation and barriers and external memory when those are what our brain needs to function well financially. The systems we've discussed throughout this book aren't crutches that make us weaker, they're appropriate accommodations that let us achieve financial stability using methods that work for how our cognitive systems actually operate rather than how financial advice assumes they should operate.

Small changes compound over time in ways that create completely different financial trajectories even though each individual change seems minor. Automating one savings transfer of two hundred dollars per payday doesn't feel dramatic, but over a year it's $5,200 we didn't have before, and over five years it's $26,000 plus whatever growth that money experiences. Canceling two forgotten subscriptions at fifteen dollars each per month saves thirty dollars monthly which is $360 per year which is $1,800 over five years. Removing shopping apps from our phone might reduce impulse purchases by a hundred dollars per month, which is $1,200 per year, which is $6,000 over five years. Each intervention individually might seem small, but together they add up to substantially different outcomes, and the beauty of these system-level changes is that they compound without requiring ongoing effort once they're established.

We're not trying to implement everything at once or to build perfect systems immediately, we're starting with whatever changes feel most achievable and building from there as those changes become established. Maybe we start by just auditing our subscriptions and canceling the ones we're definitely not using, and that's enough for now. Maybe we start by setting up one automated savings transfer and removing one shopping app, and we see how that goes before adding more changes. The approach doesn't have to be comprehensive to be valuable, even one or two system changes can make meaningful differences in how much money we retain and how much financial stress we experience, and we can always add more structure later once we've seen that initial changes actually work.

We're not broken, we just need different tools than what standard financial advice provides. Our brains work differently in ways that make certain financial tasks harder, and those differences are real and legitimate and not something we can simply overcome through greater effort or stronger commitment. What we can do is build systems that work with our brains rather than against them, that automate what we can't reliably remember, that create barriers where our impulse control fails, that remove decisions we're not equipped to make well repeatedly, that provide external memory for information our internal memory can't hold. These systems aren't perfect and they won't solve every financial challenge, but they're good enough to create stability where there was chaos, to stop the constant drain of money we couldn't account for, to build savings where before we were just trying to survive each month.

The promise here isn't transformation into someone different, it's infrastructure that works for who we actually are. Not becoming naturally disciplined, just having automation that doesn't require discipline. Not developing perfect memory, just having external systems that remember for us. Not somehow acquiring unlimited willpower, just having barriers that don't depend on willpower. We can be exactly who we are with all our cognitive quirks and limitations and still achieve financial stability through appropriate tools and structure, and that's a fundamentally more sustainable and more compassionate approach than continuing to believe that we just need to try harder at being someone we're not.

Don't miss out!

Visit the website below and you can sign up to receive emails whenever Matthew Thomas publishes a new book. There's no charge and no obligation.

https://books2read.com/r/B-A-ICCIF-LBOCJ

BOOKS 2 READ

Connecting independent readers to independent writers.

Did you love *The Spending Loop: Understanding Why We Buy and How to Finally Stop*? Then you should read *How to Pay Off Debt Fast: A 12-Month Plan to Get Rid of Credit Card Debt, Pay Down Loans, and Break the Paycheck-to-Paycheck Cycle*[1] by Amy Sheridan!

[2]

You're not bad with money. You're drowning in a system that sets you up to fail. If you're overwhelmed by bills, minimum payments, collections, or payday loans... this book is your lifeline.

Crush Your Debt (Even If You're Drowning) is a straight-talking, judgment-free guide for people who need real help with real debt. No budgeting apps. No shame. No "just stop spending on coffee" advice. Just proven strategies that actually work — even if your account is already overdrawn and you're avoiding your mail.

Inside, you'll learn exactly how to take control of your money — even if you're months behind. You'll get a step-by-step breakdown of how to prioritize bills when you can't pay them all, deal with aggressive collectors, stop the debt

1. https://books2read.com/u/mVJ9dM
2. https://books2read.com/u/mVJ9dM

snowball from growing, and take back your peace of mind. Whether you're buried under credit card debt, medical bills, personal loans, or all of the above — you'll find tools here that are simple, fast, and doable in real life.

This book is made for the financial rock bottom moments — when you're scared, exhausted, and stuck. You'll learn how to cut through the noise, stop the bleeding, and get back to breathing. And once you're stable? You'll get tools to rebuild: a simple plan to stay on track, rebuild credit, and never feel this powerless again.

If you've ever cried over a bill, panicked at the grocery store, or wondered if you'll ever get out of this hole — you don't need more guilt. You need a system that works, and a path forward that makes sense.

Approx. length: 25,000 wordsPerfect for readers of *The Total Money Makeover*, *You Need a Budget*, *The Financial Diet*, and *I Will Teach You to Be Rich* — but written for real-world crisis mode.

www.ingramcontent.com/pod-product-compliance
Lightning Source LLC
LaVergne TN
LVHW101616210926
848480LV00009B/680